About the Author

Danielle Maupertuis is a Belgian Pastry Chef who has worked in five-star hotels, abroad and in the U.K. She won several gold and silver medals in international competitions. She is one of the first Pastry Chefs to create a range of vegan desserts focused upon taste and presentation. She runs classes for amateurs and Chefs at the Vegetarian Society Cookery School. Her challenge is to give vegan desserts a fine dining touch and penetrate the exciting world of culinary awards. Writer in vegan magazines, she also gives TV cooking demos, online courses and talks in vegan shows.

Vegans Deserve Better Than a Fruit Salad

Danielle Maupertuis

Vegans Deserve Better Than a Fruit Salad

Olympia Publishers
London

www.olympiapublishers.com
OLYMPIA PAPERBACK EDITION

A CIP catalogue record for this title is
available from the British Library.

ISBN: 978-1-78830-701-7

First Published in 2020
Tallis House
2 Tallis Street
London
EC4Y 0AB
Printed in Great Britain

Dedication

To Arun, for his courage and tenacity.

Contents

Tarts, Cakes and Gateaux

Mini Cakes and Petits Fours

Festive Desserts

Christmas

Easter

Basics

Creams

INTRODUCTION

About me...

My name is Danielle Maupertuis, I am a Belgian Pastry Chef (I was baptised in chocolate!). I worked for five-star hotels abroad and in the UK. Six years in Greece as Pastry Chef for a chain of Belgian Pastry shops, six years in Lebanon as Executive Pastry Chef for the five-star Beirut Marriott hotel (with daily electricity cuts, we prepared our first wedding banquet by candlelight!) Five years in the five-star Marriott Hanbury Manor (Herts) and six years for the luxury Red Carnation hotels in London, where I received the title of "Pastry Chef of the Year". I won several gold and silver medals in culinary competitions (Wonderful plated desserts, buffets, petits fours... but that is another story!)

More and more people suffer from a food allergy, or follow an ethical philosophy, or are just concerned by healthy food options. The food industry proposes a very poor and disappointing alternative. As a Pastry Chef, I have been seriously struggling to give our customers a decent choice. Vegan guests in hotels, restaurants and coffee shops, feel very frustrated when it comes to desserts. When a choice is offered (and usually it consists of a fruit salad or sorbet!), it still suffers from poor presentation and disappointing taste.

This was until I decided to create my own range of "free from" desserts, focused upon taste and presentation. My challenge, as a Pastry Chef, is to convince people that *Vegan desserts are easy to make, taste yummy and look fantastic!*

This is why I wrote this book. It is inspired by the contents of a classical pastry book including the basics, so often neglected in existing vegan cooking literature. Inspired by classical and modern desserts from the UK and abroad, you will find a recipe for every special occasion — birthdays, afternoon teas, plated desserts, petits fours…

Activities

- Tutor at the Vegetarian Society Cookery School, where I teach vegan pastry for Chefs, as part of their week-long professional Chef's Diploma.
- Writer in vegan magazines (Vegan Living, Simply Vegan)
- Demos and talks in vegan Shows (VegFest, Vegan Life live)
- TV cooking demos (S:pprememasterTV)
- Online courses

Social Media

- https://www.freefromdesserts.com
- https://www.facebook.com/freefromdesserts
- https://www.instagram.com/dmaupertuis
- https://www.LinkedIn.com/daniellemaupertuis

About Pastry...

Pastry is a world of magic! Look how these cocoa beans grown thousands of miles away from us end up as a sophisticated chocolate praline!

Pastry is a world of precision and techniques! How many times did I hear Chefs complaining pastry is nothing without a scale and precision? True! Bread or croissants will be a disaster if you don't respect the right proving time. Chocolate and sugar need an accurate thermometer to reveal their secrets.

But — and because of these restrictions — pastry is the world of creativity and imagination.

Once you have mastered your technical barriers, you can just fly away, exploring new taste and texture combinations, new shapes and decorations. Or you can revisit some classical icons and give them a modern twist.

Finally, pastry is a lesson of humility. Of course, all these masterpieces will be captured in digital moments or pictures. But the crazy hours of trials, patience and stress, fatigue and joy will disappear in fugitive memories.

Pastry is an ephemeral art'!

About this book

Some recipes might look quite elaborate, this is part of my purpose. Inviting readers to go a step ahead, making sure they always learn something new.

I tried to make this book as didactic as my pastry lessons.

You will find lots of Chef's tips, anticipating most of the questions brought up by a recipe.

Having said this, you will always have the choice to simplify a recipe. An opera cake without the chocolate decoration is still an opera cake, with its fantastic combination of textures, colours and flavours!

Many recipes in this book are gluten free. Some of them are flourless, or you can replace the plain flour with gluten free flour. In this case, it is often recommended to add some xanthan gum.

I also brought special attention to the Basics. They should be used as a guide and a reference. And once you feel comfortable, you will be able to play around and create your own recipes!

I hope this book will contribute to sharing my passion for vegan pastry!

Cheesecakes

Red Berries Cheesecake

This colourful and refreshing cheesecake will be the main attraction of your party!

Now, let's share this second tip: Decorated with some holly leaves biscuits, it will give this cake a wonderful Christmas touch!

🍽 12 People - Loose bottom springform tin 23cm diameter
⏱ 40 Minutes preparation time
⏱ 5 Minutes cooking time

CHEESECAKE BASE

- 100g vegan spread or coconut oil
- 240g vegan digestive biscuits

METHOD

1. Line the base of a 23cm springform tin by putting a round piece of parchment paper — same size — in the bottom of the tin base.
2. Melt the spread or oil in the microwave for 20 seconds on medium power, 350 W. Grind the biscuits in a food processor. Transfer in a bowl and mix in the melted spread or oil with a spatula.
3. Press the mix into the bottom of the mould, 4 mm thick.
4. Transfer to the fridge, allowing the vegan spread or oil to harden.

CHEESECAKE MIX

- 300g soya or oat cream
- 150g golden caster sugar
- 900g hard vegan cream cheese
- 300g cranberry juice
- 3 tsp agar agar powder or 3 tbsp agar agar flakes
- 400g fresh fruits (pomegranate, blueberries, strawberries…)

METHOD

1. Dissolve the agar agar in the cranberry juice. Bring to the boil, whisking continuously. Keep it boiling for another 20 seconds.
2. Bring the cream and sugar to the boil. Add the cranberry and agar agar. On low heat, reduce 'til half of the initial quantity, whisking constantly. Allow to cool down.
3. In a mixing bowl, using the paddle attachment, beat the cream cheese at medium speed for 1 minute. Reduce the speed, add the rest of the ingredients and beat until a silky and smooth consistency. Scrape the sides and bottom of the bowl at least twice to avoid any lumps.
4. Pour the mix on top of the cheesecake base.
5. Let the cheesecake set in the freezer for about 3–4 hours.
6. Remove from the tin, decorate with red fruits, blueberries and optionally, sprinkle with some icing sugar.
7. Let it defrost at room temperature for about 1 hour.

Chef's tips

If you want to give this cheesecake a festive touch you can decorate the side with some holly leaves tuiles.

1. *Start with making a small template: Using a holly leave cutter, draw the shape on a cardboard. Cut out the shape.*
2. *Prepare a tuile mix.*
3. *Place your template on a silicone mat and spread the tuile mix with a palette knife.*
4. *Bake in a pre-heated oven at 175C for 3-4minutes.*
5. *Optionally, finish the holly leave with a little red marzipan dot.*

TUILE MIX

- 35g plain flour
- 25g icing sugar
- 30g reduced aquafaba (see Basics)
- 25g vegan spread

METHOD

1. Line the base of a 23cm springform tin by putting a round piece of parchment paper — same size — in the bottom of the tin base.
2. Melt the spread or oil in the microwave for 20 seconds on medium power, 350 W. Grind the biscuits in a food processor. Transfer in a bowl and mix in the melted spread or oil with a spatula.
3. Press the mix into the bottom of the mould, 4 mm thick.
4. Transfer to the fridge, allowing the vegan spread or oil to harden.

Pumpkin Cheesecake

Halloween is one of my favourite festive themes: bat cookies, chocolate witch hats, sweet red pepper panna cottas... and, on top of all this amazing pumpkin cheesecake! It wouldn't be the same without these little marzipan pumpkins, so I explained in detail how to make them — piece of cake!

🍽 12 People - Loose bottom springform tin 23cm diameter

⏱ 40 Minutes preparation time

⏱ 5 Minutes + 1 hour cooking time

CHEESECAKE BASE

- 75g vegan spread or coconut oil
- 200g vegan digestive biscuits

METHOD

1. Turn on the oven 190oC/gas mark 5.
2. Line the base of a 23cm loose bottom springform tin by putting a round piece of parchment paper — same size — in the bottom of the tin base.
3. Melt the spread or oil in the microwave for 20 seconds on medium power, 350 W. Grind the biscuits in a food processor. Transfer into a bowl and mix in the melted spread or oil with a spatula.
4. Press the mix into the bottom of the mould, 4 mm thick.
5. Pre bake for 5 minutes at 190oC.
6. Allow to cool down.

CHEESECAKE MIX

- 2 ½ tbsp flaxseeds mix
- 450g hard vegan cream cheese
- 425g pumpkin purée
- 210g golden caster sugar
- 1 tsp ginger
- 1 tsp cinnamon
- 1 pinch nutmeg
- 120g milk alternative

METHOD

1. Firstly, prepare the flaxseeds mix: Mix 10g of ground flaxseeds with 30g of cold water and let it rest for 10 minutes at least, until you obtain a thick purée. Keep refrigerated.

2. In a mixing bowl, fitted with the paddle attachment, beat the cream cheese at medium-low speed until creamy, for about 1 minute. Reduce the speed and gradually add the pumpkin purée, the sugar, the spices and finally the milk alternative. Increase the speed, scraping down the sides of the bowl at least twice, until it is a smooth consistency, with no remaining lumps.

3. Pour the mix over the cheesecake base, and bake at 175oC/gas mark 4 for about 1hour. (If you gently shake the tin, the filling should have a slight wobble.)

4. Let it cool down for 2 hours at least, before removing from the mould. Slide the parchment paper out from underneath and transfer to a plate.

DECORATION

Marzipan pumpkins

1. Using plastic gloves, colour 200g of a marzipan block in orange and 50g in dark green.
2. Divide the orange marzipan into 12 pieces, about 15g each.
3. Roll each piece into a round shape.
4. With a toothpick, press some lines from top to bottom to reproduce a pumpkin shape.
5. Between 2 pieces of parchment paper, roll out the green marzipan, 2mm thick. Using a star nozzle, cut 12 pieces and place each one on top of the pumpkin.
6. 6. Finish with a little stem.

Sweet pastry bases

1. Prepare a sweet pastry as explained in the Basics.
2. Roll out the pastry between 2 pieces of parchment paper, 2 mm thick. With a round cutter, cut 12 discs, 2.5cm diameter.
3. Place on a pre-lined baking tray and bake at 175oC/gas mark 4 for 8 minutes.
4. Put the marzipan pumpkins on top of the sweet pastry bases and place equally onto the cheesecake.

Pomegranate Cheesecake

When you work on a dessert presentation, the shape you choose will certainly be a significant part of the job.

As you will see, I am using a lot of shapes in my recipes. You will find some useful addresses at the end of this book. Instead of starting with the cheesecake base, the pomegranate jelly will be the first step in the assembling of the cake. Unusual to work upside down, isn't it?

And I haven't mentioned the numerous pomegranate health benefits…

🍽 6 Pyramids - 7 x 7cm base

⏱ 30 Minutes preparation time

⏱ 2 Hours to set

CHEESECAKE BASE

- 30g vegan spread or coconut oil
- 70g vegan digestive biscuits

METHOD

1. Melt the spread or oil in the microwave for 20 seconds. Grind the biscuits in a food processor. Transfer into a bowl and mix in the melted spread or oil with a spatula.
2. Roll out between 2 sheets of parchment paper, 3mm thick. Transfer to a flat tray and keep in the fridge, allowing the vegan spread or oil to harden.

CHEESECAKE MIX

- 180g pomegranate juice
- 1 ¾ tsp agar agar powder or 1 ¾ tbsp agar flakes
- 150g soya or oat cream
- 90g golden caster sugar
- 120g vegan Greek style cheese
- 180g vegan cream cheese
- vegan friendly red food colouring or beetroot juice (optional)

METHOD

1. Dissolve the agar agar in the pomegranate juice and bring to the boil, whisking continuously. Keep it boiling for about 20 seconds.
2. Add the cream and bring it back to the boil. On medium heat, gently reduce until half of the initial quantity remains, stirring constantly.
3. In a mixing bowl, fitted with the paddle attachment, beat the sugar, cream cheese and the Greek style cheese at medium-high speed until creamy, for about 2 minutes.
4. Reduce the speed and gradually add the reduced pomegranate mix.
5. Increase the speed, scraping down the sides of the bowl twice at least, until a smooth consistency, with no remaining lumps.

POMEGRANATE JELLY

- 120g pomegranate juice
- ½ tsp agar agar powder or ½ tbsp agar flakes
- seeds of a whole pomegranate fruit

METHOD

1. Dissolve the agar agar in the pomegranate juice. Bring to the boil and keep boiling for 20 seconds.

ASSEMBLING

1. Keeping your mould upside down, pour 1 generous tsp of pomegranate seeds into the bottom of each pyramid mould. Cover the seeds with the jelly.
2. They will set at room temperature or, for a quicker result, transfer to the freezer for 1 hour.
3. Fill the mould with the cheesecake mix. Leave ½ cm free on the top to place the cheesecake base. Put back in the freezer for 1h at least.
4. Remove the cheesecake base from the fridge. Cut the bases same size as the mould, put on top and let it set for another 2 hours in the freezer.
5. Remove the cakes from the mould and let them defrost at room temperature for about 20 minutes.

Mango and Passion Fruit Cheesecake

Bored with fruit salads? These little verrines will be ideal for picnics and barbecues. The fresh tang of passion fruit and mango will be an ideal combination during hot weather.

And in these little jars, there is no risk of the cream collapsing!

🍴 5 Jars - 4cm diameter, 8cm high - 75ml
⏱ 30 Minutes preparation time
⏱ 2 Hours to set

CHEESECAKE BASE

- 15g vegan spread or coconut oil
- 40g vegan digestive biscuits

METHOD

1. Melt the spread or oil in the microwave for 20 seconds medium power 350 W. Grind the biscuits in a food processor. Transfer into a bowl and mix in the melted spread or oil with a spatula.
2. Using a pestle or anything heavy, press the mix into the bottom of the jar, 5 mm thick.
3. Transfer to the fridge, allowing the vegan spread or oil to harden.

CHEESECAKE MIX

- 180g mango purée (made from very ripe mangoes)
- 1 tsp agar agar powder or 1 tbsp agar flakes
- 25g unrefined golden caster sugar
- 150g vegan cream cheese
- 40g oat cream

METHOD

1. Purée the mango in a blender. If necessary, add 1–2 tbsp of water to make the first pulse easier.
2. In a saucepan, dissolve the agar agar in the fruit purée. Bring to the boil, whisking continuously and keep it boiling for 20 seconds.
3. Pour the rest of the ingredients into a food processor. Slowly add the purée and blend until it's a smooth and silky consistency.
4. Fill the jar with the mix and leave 1cm space at the top.
5. Transfer to the freezer for at least 1 hour.

FRUIT JELLY

*   100g mango and passionfruit juice
*   ½ tsp agar agar powder or ½ tbsp agar flakes
*   1-2 fresh passion fruits

METHOD

1. Dissolve the agar agar in the juice and bring to the boil, whisking continuously. Keep it boiling for about 20 seconds.
2. Take the jar from the freezer, spread a few passion fruits seeds over the mix, and pour the jelly on top of it.
3. Let it set in the fridge.

Peanut Butter Cheesecake

Here we are just having fun playing with all these different textures: a soft cheesecake biscuit base, crispy caramelised nuts and seeds, a smooth chocolate cream, and layers of crunchy peanut butter cheesecake.

🍽 5 Jars 4cm diameter, 8cm high - 75ml

⏱ 30 Minutes preparation time

⏱ 1 Hour to set

CHEESECAKE BASE

- 15g vegan spread or coconut oil
- 40g vegan digestive biscuits

METHOD

1. Melt the spread or oil in the microwave for 20 seconds. Grind the biscuits in a food processor. Transfer into a bowl and mix in the melted spread or oil with a spatula.
2. Using a pestle or anything heavy, press the mix into the bottom of the jar, 5 mm thick.
3. Transfer to the fridge, allowing the vegan spread or oil to harden.

CHEESECAKE MIX

- 1 tsp agar agar powder or 1 tbsp agar flakes
- 50g soya or oat cream
- 50g golden caster sugar
- 60g vegan Greek style cheese
- 100g vegan cream cheese
- 50g vegan crunchy peanut butter

METHOD

1. Dissolve the agar agar in the cream. Bring to the boil, whisking continuously and keep it boiling for about 20 seconds.
2. Pour the rest of the ingredients into a food processor. Add the agar agar and cream.
3. Blend until it's a smooth and silky consistency.
4. Pour the cheesecake mix over the crust. Fill the jar half full and let it set at room temperature or, for a quicker result, in the freezer for ½ h.

CARAMELISED NUTS AND SEEDS

*   100g unrefined caster sugar
*   60g mixed nuts and seeds (hazelnuts, walnuts, pumpkin seeds, sesame …)

METHOD

1. Crush the nuts and seeds — just a few pulses in the food processor.
2. Sprinkle them generously on a silicone mat or baking paper.
3. Bring the sugar slowly to a caramel stage — 165oC if using a sugar thermometer. Avoid stirring. Pour it cautiously over the dry fruits.
4. Allow to cool down and crush them in the food processor.

CHOCOLATE GANACHE

- 50g vegan dark chocolate chips
- 40g oat or soya cream
- 10g milk alternative

METHOD

1. In a heavy bottom saucepan, bring the cream and milk to the boil, pour the chocolate chips and whisk until it's a smooth consistency.

ASSEMBLING

1. Generously sprinkle some nuts over half the cheesecake mix.
2. Cover with a second layer of cheesecake mix, transfer back to the fridge.
3. Pour some ganache on top, let it set and finish with some nuts.

Chocolate
Desserts

Chocolate and Clementine Tartlets

When it comes to chocolate, orange or clementine is one of the best combos.The light acidity of the clementine is balanced with the soft texture of the chocolate cream, while the clementine mousseline equilibrates the overwhelming power of the chocolate.

🍴 6 Tartlets, 10 cm diameter

⏱ 45 Minutes preparation time

⏱ 2 Hours to set

⏱ 20 Minutes cooking time

CHOCOLATE SWEET PASTRY

- 75g vegan spread
- 100g golden caster sugar or icing sugar
- 40g milk alternative
- 165g plain flour
- 20g unsweetened vegan cocoa powder
- ¾ tsp baking powder

METHOD

1. In a mixing bowl, using the paddle attachment, beat the spread and the sugar at medium speed, until you reach a fluffy consistency. Reduce the speed and slowly pour in the milk alternative.

2. Add the flour, cocoa powder and baking powder. Work on a low speed until all the ingredients are combined. Do not overwork the pastry.

3. Cling film the pastry and allow to rest in the fridge, ideally overnight or at least 2hours the same day.

4. Preheat the oven to 190oC/gas mark 5.

5. On a lightly floured work surface, roll out the pastry and use to line 6 tartlet tins 10cm diameter. Trim off the excess and line with a piece of cling film. Fill with baking beans or rice, and bake in the oven for 12 minutes. Remove the beans and cling film. Reduce the temperature to 175oC and put the tartlets back in the oven for 8 minutes. Take out of the tin and put on a wire rack to cool completely.

CHOCOLATE CLEMENTINE GANACHE

- 60g vegan dark chocolate 52%
- 30g vegan milk chocolate
- 50g oat cream
- 20g milk alternative
- 1 tbsp clementine zest

METHOD

1. Break the chocolates into pieces, and melt cautiously in the microwave on medium power, 350W, 15 seconds at a time.
2. In a heavy bottom saucepan, bring the cream and milk alternative to the boil, pour in the melted chocolates and clementine zest, stir until it's a smooth consistency.
3. Allow to cool down until a medium hard consistency is reached, ready to pipe.

CLEMENTINE MOUSSELINE

- 125g milk alternative
- 125g clementine juice
- 30g cornflour
- 50g golden caster sugar
- 1 ½ tbsp cashew butter
- 1 tbsp clementine zest
- 50g vegan spread

METHOD

1. In a heavy bottom saucepan pour the milk alternative and the clementine juice, reserve 3 tbsp to be added to the dry ingredients and bring to the boil.
2. Meanwhile, in a bowl, with an electric hand mixer, whisk together the cashew butter, sugar, cornflour, zest and the reserved liquid.
3. Away from the heat, pour this mix over the boiling milk/juice and whisk until all the ingredients are evenly combined.

4. Bring back to a low heat and stir continuously until the mixture starts bubbling and thickens.
5. Add the spread and give it a last whisk. Allow to cool.

ASSEMBLING

1. Deposit 60g of the clementine mousseline in the bottom of each tartlet.
2. Pour the ganache into a piping bag. Using a plain nozzle, pipe some dots all around the tartlets.
3. Garnish the centre with some clementines cut in half.
4. Glaze the fruits with some warmed apricot glaze.

Chocolate Saint-Honorè

This classic French dessert is named after Bishop Honoratus, patron saint of bakers and pastry chefs.

I can't tell you how many times I tried vegan choux pastry recipes, before getting a satisfying result.

But now, I see you salivating already! This cake should be eaten the same day. Is it a problem?

🍽 6 St Honore , 8cm diameter (24 choux pastry pieces)
⏱ 40 Minutes preparation time
⏱ 5 Minutes + 35 minutes cooking time
⏱ ½ Hour extra time to rest

PUFF PASTRY

1. Prepare a puff pastry as explained in the Basics.
2. On a lightly floured worktop, roll out the pastry, 3mm thick. Cut out 6 discs 8cm diameter, transfer onto a pre-lined baking tray and let them rest for about ½ hour.
3. In the meantime, preheat the oven to 205oC/gas mark 6. Bake the disks for 15 minutes.

CHOUX PASTRY

*   125g milk alternative
*   40g vegan spread
*   70g plain flour
*   1 ½ tsp baking powder
*   1 tsp apple cider vinegar
*   3tbsp vegan egg powder " Follow your heart "
*   180g iced cold water
*   40g reduced aquafaba (see Basics)

METHOD

1. Prepare a choux pastry as explained in the Basics.
2. Pour the choux pastry into a piping bag, using a plain nozzle 12mm diameter. On a silicone mat, pipe 24 little choux. Brush them with some milk alternative + soft brown sugar, the vegan egg wash substitute.
3. Keeping the oven temperature at 205oC, bake for 15 minutes, then reduce to 175oC and bake for another 20 minutes.

CHOCOLATE CREAM

- 250g milk alternative
- 50g golden caster sugar
- 25g corn flour
- 1 tsp cashew butter
- a few drops of vanilla essence
- 20g vegan spread
- 75g vegan dark chocolate chips

METHOD

1. Prepare a custard as explained in the Basics.
2. Add the chocolate chips while the custard is still warm. Give the cream a whisk until all the chocolate has been evenly incorporated. Allow to cool down.

CHOCOLATE GANACHE

- 160g oat cream
- 40g milk alternative
- 200g vegan dark chocolate chips

METHOD

1. In a heavy bottom saucepan, bring the cream and milk alternative to the boil.
2. Add the chocolate chips and stir until it's a smooth and velvety texture.
3. Keep it warm and runny.

ASSEMBLING

1. Pour the chocolate cream into a piping bag, using a plain nozzle 5mm diameter.
2. Make a small hole in the bottom of the choux with a knife.
3. Generously fill the choux with the chocolate cream.
4. Dip each choux into the chocolate ganache and transfer them to a rack. Let them set at room temperature.
5. Display the 6 puff pastry bases and place 3 choux on each, at equal distance.
6. Using a star nozzle 12mm diameter, nicely pipe some cream in the middle and in between each choux. Stack a last choux on top of the middle cream.

Chocolate and Orange Dome

Like a Kinder chocolate, you will be surprised to bite into this moist orange cake, hidden in a light chocolate mousse.
The great advantage of this cake is it can be entirely prepared in advance and kept in the freezer.

You can also enjoy these orange cakes separately as little bites.

🍽 6 Half spheres 8cm diameter

⏱ 40 Minutes preparation time

⏱ 15 Minutes cooking time

ORANGE CAKE

- 45g reduced aquafaba (see Basics)
- 45g unrefined caster sugar
- 45g melted vegan spread
- 25g plain flour
- 10g cornflour
- 15g ground almonds
- 2 organic orange zests

METHOD

1. Preheat the oven 190oC, gas mark 5.
2. In a very clean mixing bowl, whisk the reduced aquafaba at high speed until soft peaks. Slowly add the sugar and whisk until it reaches stiff peaks.
3. Reduce to low speed and slowly add the melted vegan spread.
4. Combine the flour, cornflour, ground almonds and orange zest in a bowl.
5. With a spatula, slowly fold the aquafaba mix into the dry ingredients.

6. Fill the little half spheres to the top of the moulds.
7. Bake for about 15 minutes at 190oC.
8. Allow them to cool down and transfer them to the freezer. They will be easier to remove from mould.

CHOCOLATE MOUSSE

- 220g vegan dark chocolate 52%
- 6 tbsp thick coconut milk (see Basics)
- 1 ripe crushed avocado
- 8 tbsp maple syrup or agave nectar
- 30g oat cream
- 60g reduced aquafaba (see Basics)

METHOD

1. Prepare a chocolate mousse as explained in the Basics.

ASSEMBLING

1. 1. Remove the orange cakes from the freezer, remove from mould.
2. 2. Using half sphere moulds 8 cm diameter, spoon the chocolate mousse up to halfway, press the orange cake in the middle and cover with chocolate mousse to the top.
3. 3. Let the domes set in the freezer. Remove from mould and let them defrost for about 1 hour before serving.

Chef's tips

You can add some crunchiness to this cake by placing a disk of chocolate sweet pastry at the bottom (see Basics).

Chocolate Cheesecake, Caramelised Nuts and Seeds

I am not sure how it sounds in English, but in French we say "Ce dessert est le Bon Dieu en culottes de velours", this dessert is "Jesus in velvet trousers"!

The refinement of this cheesecake is to surprise our palate with this milk chocolate ganache, a velvety cushion between the dark chocolate cheesecake and the caramelised nuts.

🍽 6-8 Square mould 18x18x4cm

⏱ 40 Minutes preparation time

⏱ 2½ Hours to set

CHEESECAKE BASE

- 60g vegan spread or coconut oil
- 160g vegan digestive biscuits

METHOD

1. Melt the vegan spread or oil in the microwave for 20 seconds. Grind the biscuits in a food processor. Transfer into a bowl and mix in the melted vegan spread or oil with a spatula.
2. Pre-line the mould with parchment paper. Press the mix into the bottom of the mould, 4–5mm thick.
3. Transfer to the fridge allowing the vegan spread or oil to harden.

CHOCOLATE CHEESECAKE MIX

- 100g agar agar mix (see Basics)
- 180g vegan dark chocolate (52% or 72%)
- 100g oat cream
- 90g golden caster sugar
- 240g vegan cream cheese

METHOD

1. Melt the chocolate in the microwave on medium power, 350W, 15 seconds at a time (temperature should not exceed 45oC). Heat up the agar agar mix until totally liquid. Whisk until smooth and silky consistency.
2. Pour the sugar, the cream and the cream cheese into a mixing bowl. Using the paddle attachment, beat the ingredients together at high speed for about 1 minute. Reduce the speed and slowly add the chocolate mix. Whisk until the cheesecake mix has a homogeneous texture with no remaining lumps.
3. Pour over the cheesecake base, leave ½ cm free at the top for the chocolate ganache.
4. Transfer to the freezer for 2 hours at least.

CHOCOLATE CHEESECAKE MIX

- 180g vegan milk chocolate
- 60g oat cream
- 25g milk alternative

METHOD

1. Break the chocolate into pieces and melt in the microwave on medium power, 350W, 15 seconds at a time
2. In a heavy bottom saucepan, bring the cream and the milk alternative to the boil, pour in the melted chocolate and whisk until it's a smooth consistency.
3. Pour the ganache evenly over the cheesecake and let it set in the fridge for ½ hour at least.

CARAMELISED NUTS AND SEEDS

- 150g unrefined caster sugar
- 75g mixed nuts and seeds (hazelnuts, walnuts, pumpkin seeds, sesame…)

METHOD

1. Crush the nuts and seeds, just a few pulses in the food processor. Sprinkle them generously on a silicone mat.
2. Bring the sugar slowly to a caramel stage. Avoid stirring. Pour it cautiously over the dry fruits.
3. Allow the caramel to harden and cut some random pieces with a knife.

ASSEMBLING

1. Let the cheesecake rest for about 1hour at room temperature to defrost.
2. Generously sprinkle some caramelised nuts over the cheesecake mix.
3. Ready to serve.

Chef's tips

If the cheesecake mix remains slightly lumpy after mixing all the ingredients, just put in the microwave for 20 seconds and give it a quick stir.

If you can find vegan chocolate chips, they are very easy to use: no need to melt in the microwave, just pour over the boiling cream and whisk.

If you are using golden caster sugar, check the temperature of the caramel with a thermometer. Because of its golden colour, the sugar reaches the caramel colour quicker than a white caster sugar. Temperature should be 165oC.

Chocolate Fondant with a Mango Coulis

This dessert is for chocoholics only! I have a special thought for them by delivering a top-secret way to guarantee this fondant a perfect bake.

The mango coulis is optional, just to add a fresh exotic touch, but I presume the chocoholics will consider it as a sin!

🍴 4 Pudding bases 175ml
⏱ 20 Minutes preparation time
⏱ 20 Minutes cooking time

CHOCOLATE GANACHES BALLS

- 60g oat cream
- 15g milk alternative
- 100g vegan dark chocolate chips

METHOD

1. In a heavy bottom saucepan bring the cream and milk alternative to the boil. Turn off the heat, incorporate the chocolate chips and stir until you reach a smooth and velvety consistency. Transfer to the fridge.
2. When the ganache is hard, roll little balls 6–8g each — depending how strong you are addicted to chocolate! Keep them in the freezer.

CHOCOLATE FONDANT

- 140g vegan dark chocolate (52% or 72%)
- 160g oat cream
- 80g maple syrup
- 50g rapeseed oil
- 100g plain flour
- Vegan spread for greasing
- Vegan cocoa powder for dusting

METHOD

1. Preheat the oven 190oC/gas mark 5.
2. Using a pastry brush, generously grease the moulds with the vegan spread. Evenly dust the inside of the moulds with cocoa powder.
3. Melt the chocolate in the microwave on medium power, 350W, 15 seconds at a time.
4. In a mixing bowl whisk together the oat cream, maple syrup and rapeseed oil. Slowly add the flour. When the mix is homogeneous, pour in the melted chocolate and whisk at medium speed until it's a smooth consistency.
5. Fill half of each mould with the fondant mix. Put a chocolate ganache ball in the middle and cover with the rest of the fondant mix. Each mould should contain 115g of the mix.
6. Bake 190oC for 20 minutes. Remove from mould while warm.

MANGO COULIS

- 1 ripe mango
- 40-60g golden caster sugar (depending on the sweetness of the fruit)
- Water

METHOD

1. Purée the fruits in a blender. If necessary, add 1– 2 tbsp of water to make the first pulse easier.
2. In a saucepan, combine the mango purée and sugar. Heat up the mix gently until the sugar is totally dissolved. Add some water until it's the desired consistency, give it a last whisk and transfer to the fridge.

PRESENTATION

On a plate, cut off about a quarter of the fondant, allowing the chocolate to run. Pour some mango coulis over the chocolate and decorate with some fresh fruits, and a mint leaf.

Trio of Chocolate Cheesecake

Elegance is the master key of this dessert, particularly appreciated in my Pastry courses, and the students are surprised to see how easy it is to temper chocolate!

🍽 6 Glasses 300ml

⏱ 1 Hour preparation time

⏱ 5½ Hours to set

CHEESECAKE BASE

- 40g vegan spread or coconut oil
- 100g vegan digestive biscuits

METHOD

1. Melt the vegan spread or oil in the microwave for 20 seconds. Grind the biscuits in a food processor. With a spatula, mix the melted spread and ground biscuits.
2. Using a pestle, or anything heavy, press the mix into the bottom of the glass, 4–5 mm thick.
3. Transfer to the fridge, allowing the vegan spread or oil to harden.

CHOCOLATE CHEESECAKE MIXES

Dark chocolate cheesecake mix:
- 140g vegan dark chocolate 72%
- 100g agar agar mix (see Basics)
- 100g oat cream
- 90g unrefined caster sugar
- 200g vegan cream cheese

Milk chocolate cheesecake mix:
- 140g vegan milk chocolate
- 100g agar agar mix (see Basics)
- 100g oat cream
- 80g unrefined caster sugar
- 200g vegan cream cheese

White chocolate cheesecake mix:
- 140g vegan white chocolate
- 100g agar agar mix (see Basics)
- 100g oat cream
- 70g unrefined caster sugar
- 200g vegan cream cheese

METHOD

1. Firstly, prepare the agar agar mix as explained in the Basics.
2. Melt the chocolate in the microwave on medium power, 350W, 15 seconds at a time. Do not overheat. (Temperature should not exceed 45oC). Keep aside.
3. In a mixing bowl pour in the oat cream, the sugar and the non-dairy cream cheese. Using the paddle attachment beat the mix at medium speed until you reach a smooth consistency.
4. Heat up 100g of the agar agar mix until totally liquid and add to the melted dark chocolate. Give it a stir and slowly add to the cheesecake mix. Again, beat until it's a smooth and silky consistency.
5. With a piping bag, pour the dark chocolate cheesecake mix into the glass, about 3 ½ cm thick. Transfer to the fridge and let it set for ½ hour.
6. Repeat the same operation with the milk and white chocolate.

DECORATION

- 150g vegan dark chocolate 52%
- 150g vegan milk chocolate
- 150g vegan white chocolate

METHOD

1. Slowly melt 150g of each chocolate in the microwave, on medium power, 350W, 15 seconds at a time and temper the chocolates as explained in the Basics.
2. With a flexible palette knife spread each chocolate onto an acetate film. Leave it to harden at room temperature and cut some random shapes, as you fancy. Store in an airtight container.

Chef's tips

If, when pouring the melted chocolate into the cheesecake mix, you get some chocolate crystals in your mix, just put back in the microwave for a few seconds. This is due to the difference of temperatures between both mixes.

English Classics
with Modern Twists

Sticky Toffee Pudding with Toffee Sauce

Do I have to introduce the Number 1, the legend of all English desserts? Some sticky toffee puddings recipes are quite heavy. I don't agree with these versions. Desserts are your last and definite impression of a meal, and we should always leave the table with a light stomach. On the contrary, in the recipe I propose, all the combined ingredients make the pudding particularly soft and fluffy. And when we start the toffee sauce, my students always double the quantities — I wonder why??

🍽 6 Pudding basins 175ml

⏱ 30 Minutes preparation time

⏱ 50 Minutes cooking time

STICKY TOFFEE PUDDING

- 190ml milk alternative (rice, coconut, almond …)
- 75ml water
- 150g chopped dates
- ¾ tsp bicarbonate of soda
- 120g light muscovado sugar
- 120g vegan spread
- 1 ½ tsp soda
- 1 ½ tsp cider vinegar
- 45g flaxseed mix
- 1 tsp cinnamon
- ¾ tsp ginger
- ¼ tsp nutmeg
- 45g water
- 30g rapeseed oil
- 150g self-raising flour
- Vegan spread for greasing

METHOD

1 day before...

1. Simmer the dates gently with the water and milk. When reaching boiling point, remove from the heat, add the soda, give a stir and let it cool down in the fridge.
2. Prepare the flaxseeds mix: Mix 20g of flaxseeds with 60g of cold water and let it set in the fridge for 15minutes at least.

Next day...

1. Preheat the oven to 175oC/Gas mark 4.
2. In a mixer, using the paddle attachment, medium speed, beat together the sugar and vegan spread until fluffy. Add the chopped dates, the soda and cider vinegar, the flaxseeds mix and the spices. Finally, incorporate the water and rapeseed oil. On a low speed, add the self-raising flour. Keep on beating until it's a smooth texture, with no remaining lumps.
3. Using a pastry brush, generously grease the inside of the basin moulds with hard vegan spread. Fill each mould with the mix, leave 1 cm free to allow the pudding to rise. Bake for 50 minutes. Remove from mould while hot.

STICKY TOFFEE PUDDING

- 75g golden unrefined caster sugar
- 25g vegan spread
- 60g oat cream
- 60g soya cream

METHOD

1. 1. In a deep and heavy bottom saucepan, melt the sugar on medium heat. Avoid stirring.
2. 2. In the meantime, warm up the creams in the microwave.
3. 3. As soon as the caramel colour is reached, take the saucepan off the heat and add the spread, stirring continuously. Slowly incorporate the creams, bring back to a medium heat and gently reduce the sauce until smooth and homogeneous.

Chef's tips

If you are using golden caster sugar, check the temperature of the caramel with a thermometer: because of its golden colour, the sugar reaches the caramel colour quicker than a white caster sugar, but is not ready yet. Make sure it gets to 165oC.

Always warm up the creams before pouring in the caramel sauce. A cold cream will crystallise the sugar and you will seriously struggle to bring it back to a homogeneous consistency.

When pouring in the caramel, the cream is bubbling vigorously so, for safety reasons, always use a deep saucepan.

Eton Mess

Here comes a tribute to classical English desserts. Rich, simple and tasty, these modern twists will definitely put them among the best of GBBO!

🍴 4 Glasses 250 ml

⏱ 40 Minutes preparation time

⏱ 1 Hour 15 minutes cooking time

MERINGUE

- 50g reduced aquafaba (see Basics)
- 90g caster sugar
- 1 tbsp dried strawberries

METHOD

1. Preheat the oven to 100C /gas mark ¼ and line a large baking tray with parchment paper or a silicone mat.
2. In a perfctly clean bowl, whisk the reduced aquafaba until it reaches soft peaks.
3. Slowly add the sugar and continue to whisk until there are stiff peaks.
4. Pour the meringue into a piping bag with a plain nozzle 10mm diameter. and pipe different shapes (long stripes, squares, rounds…). Sprinkle the meringue with some dried strawberries.
5. Place on a baking tray and bake until the meringues are completely hard and come off the paper or the mat easily. The baking time depends on the size and thickness of the meringue, about 30 minutes. for the thin stripes to 1 hour–1 hour 15 minutes for the bigger squares or discs.
6. Allow them to cool down for about 10 minutes before taking them off the tray.

STRAWBERRY COMPOTE

- 50g reduced aquafaba (see Basics)
- 90g caster sugar
- 1 tbsp dried strawberries

METHOD

1. Wash the strawberries, discard the green stalk and cut them into 4 pieces.
2. Bring the strawberries and sugar to the boil, let it gently simmer and reduce on a low heat until it becomes a syrupy consistency.
3. Allow to cool down and transfer to the fridge.

COCONUT WHIPPED CREAM

- 2 cans full fat coconut milk (at least 52% coconut fat)
- 4 tbsp maple syrup (or corn or agave syrup)
- 1 tbsp vanilla extract

METHOD

1. Prepare the coconut whipped cream as explained in the Basics.

ASSEMBLING

1. Tip the meringue pieces into the glasses with some fresh strawberries, pipe the whipped cream and thoroughly swirl the strawberry compote. Finish with the meringue sticks.

Bread and Butter Pudding with Pecans and Apricots

Some people might think bread and butter pudding is a common, poor and boring dessert.

A quick look at this recipe, and I am sure they will change their mind! A rich brioche is soaked in a runny custard sauce and sprinkled with coconut sugar. The dry fruits and nuts bringing some crunchiness. If this is still not convincing, some edible flowers will make the difference!

🍽 2   Casseroles 6cm x 10cm diameter

⏱ 30   Minutes preparation time

⏱ 40-45 Minutes cooking time

VANILLA SAUCE

- 125g milk alternative
- 20g golden caster sugar
- 12g cornflour
- 1 tsp cashew butter
- ½ vanilla bean
- vegan friendly yellow food colouring
- 50g oat cream
- 50g milk alternative

METHOD

1. Prepare a custard cream as explained in the Basics. Let it cool down. Pour the cream and milk alternative into the custard and whisk until smooth.

BREAD AND BUTTER PUDDING

- 6 slices of a vegan bread loaf or brioche
- 60g dried apricots
- 40g crushed pecan nuts
- 2 tbsp coconut sugar
- 2 tbsp apricot jam

METHOD

1. Soak the dried apricots in warm water for 2 hours at least. Dry them in a clean tea towel, and cut them into chunks.
2. Preheat the oven 160oC/gas mark 3.
3. Cut 6 discs in the brioche or loaf slices, same size as the casseroles.
4. Soak the first disc in the vanilla sauce for about 2 minutes and place it in the bottom of the cassolette. Spread ½ tsp of apricot jam on the brioche and sprinkle some coconut sugar, apricot chunks and crushed pecans.
5. Repeat these steps a second time. Finish with a layer of brioche and pour the remaining sauce evenly over the pudding. Do not put the apricots and pecans in yet, as they would burn during the baking.
6. Bake in a bain-marie for about 40 minutes. Sprinkle with coconut sugar, apricots, pecans and optionally some edible flowers.

Rhubarb and Raspberry Summer Pudding with a White Chocolate Sauce

The best rhubarb is the "spring pudding", growing and ready early spring. I present here a very simple way to make the pudding and, for me, it's even better than the traditional version where the bread often overpowers the taste of the fruits.

The white chocolate sauce is a must if you want to appreciate the rhubarb at its best…

🍽 6 Rings 7cm diameter

⏱ 20 Minutes preparation time

⏱ 10-15 Minutes cooking time

RHUBARB AND RASPBERRY PUDDING

- 500g fresh rhubarb
- 2 punnets of fresh raspberries
- 3 tbsp water
- 150g + 50g unrefined caster sugar, or coconut sugar
- 2 pinches of ground ginger
- 1 loaf of vegan sliced bread or brioche

METHOD

1. Preheat the oven 170oC/gas mark 4.
2. Wash the rhubarb stalks and cut them in pieces 2cm length. Line a baking tray with parchment paper or a silicone mat. Arrange the rhubarb pieces on the tray. Generously sprinkle with the 150g of sugar and optionally 1 or 2 pinches of ground ginger. Bake for 10–15 minutes at 170oC. Pass the rhubarb through a sieve. Transfer to a bowl and add 1 punnet of raspberries.

RASPBERRY COULIS

- 1 punnet raspberries
- 50g golden caster sugar
- 3 tbsp water

METHOD

1. Pour all the ingredients together into a saucepan. Bring the fruits slowly to the boil, reduce the heat and let them gently simmer for another 2–3 minutes. Take off the heat and allow to cool down. Purée the fruits in a blender.

WHITE CHOCOLATE SAUCE

- 100g vegan white chocolate
- 100g oat cream
- 1 tbsp dried raspberries

METHOD

1. Melt the chocolate in the microwave on medium power, 350W, 15 seconds at a time. In the meantime, bring 100g vegan alternative cream (oat cream, coconut cream …) to the boil and pour into the melted chocolate. Whisk until it's a smooth consistency. Decorate the plate and sprinkle on some dried raspberries.

ASSEMBLING

1. Prepare 6 stainless rings 7 cm (2 ¾ inches). Cut the crusts off the bread. For each pudding, using biscuit cutters, stamp out 2 circles of the same diameter as the ring.
2. Start to build up the pudding. Firstly, dip 6 circles of bread one at a time into the juice for a few seconds, just to coat. Push each circle into the bottom of the ring.
3. Spoon in the rhubarb and raspberries and top with the remaining 6 circles dipped in the juice as well. Cover with cling film and put a weight (such as a jar of jam) on top. Chill for 6 hours or overnight.
4. To serve the puddings, uncover, run a knife around the edge and remove the ring.
5. Serve with the remaining juice, ice cream or white chocolate sauce.

Doughnut Rings

Among my neighbours and family who regularly get to sample my creations, these doughnuts instantly became a star, loved by kids and adults! Custard, chocolate, salted caramel, what else can we dream of?

🍽 10 Pieces, 8cm diameter

⏱ 20 Minutes preparation time

⏱ 2 Hours 20 minutes cooking time

DOUGHNUT DOUGH

- 165g plain flour
- 3 tsp dry yeast
- 180g lukewarm water
- 1 tbsp caster sugar
- 165g strong white flour
- 45g melted vegan spread
- ¾ tsp baking powder
- ¾ tsp salt

METHOD

1. Prepare a doughnut dough as explained in the previous recipe.
2. Transfer the dough onto a slightly floured worktop. Knock the dough back and roll it into a rectangle 2 cm thick. With a cutter, cut 10 round shapes 8 cm diameter, then cut a hole in the centre 3cm diameter. Place them onto a floured baking tray. Cover with a tea towel and leave for about 1 hour, until doubled in size.
3. Fill your deep-fat fryer or heavy-based saucepan halfway with oil. Heat the oil to 180oC. When the oil is heated, carefully slide the doughnuts from the tray using a floured pastry scraper. Taking care not to deflate them, put them into the oil. Do 2–3 per batch. Fry for 2 minutes each side until golden brown.

4. Remove the doughnuts from the fryer and place them onto a kitchen paper. Repeat the steps until all the doughnuts are fried, but keep checking the oil temperature is correct. Set aside to cool before filling.

FILLINGS

Cut the doughnuts in half. Fill a piping bag with the filling of your choice. Pipe evenly half of the doughnut and cover with the second half.

LIGHT COCONUT CUSTARD

- 250g milk alternative
- 50g caster sugar
- 25g corn flour
- 1tbsp cashew butter
- a few drops of vanilla essence
- Yellow vegan friendly food colouring (optional)
- Coconut whipped cream (see Basics)

METHOD

1. Prepare a custard as explained in the Basics. Allow to cool down.

VANILLA FILLING

- 20g coconut whipped cream
- 60g light coconut custard

METHOD

1. Incorporate the coconut whipped cream with the light coconut custard.
2. Whisk with an electric hand mixer until smooth and velvety.
3. Lightly spray the doughnuts with some rapeseed oil and sprinkle some caster sugar on top.

CHOCOLATE FILLING

- 50g dark chocolate
- 20g coconut whipped cream
- 60g light coconut custard

METHOD

1. Whisk 50g dark chocolate into the milk.
2. Incorporate the coconut whipped cream with the light coconut custard.
3. Whisk with an electric hand mixer until smooth and velvety.

SALTED CARAMEL FILLING

- 30g salted caramel
- 45g coconut whipped cream
- 60g light coconut custard

METHOD

1. Incorporate the coconut whipped cream with the light coconut custard.
2. Whisk with an electric hand mixer until smooth and velvety.
3. Add 30g salted caramel and give it a last whisk.

TOPPINGS

CHOCOLATE

- 80g oat cream
- 20g milk alternative
- 100g vegan dark chocolate chips

METHOD

1. Pour the cream and milk into a heavy bottom saucepan and bring to the boil. Take off the heat, add the chocolate chips and stir until you reach a velvety consistency.

SALTED CARAMEL

- 75g caster sugar
- 25g vegan spread
- 50g oat cream

METHOD

1. In a heavy bottom saucepan, bring the sugar gently to a caramel stage — 165oC if using a sugar thermometer. Avoid stirring.
2. In the meantime, warm up the cream in the microwave.
3. When the sugar reaches a caramel colour, remove from the heat, add the spread and stir until total absorption. Incorporate the warm cream and stir until a homogeneous consistency. Bring back to the heat and give it a last whisk.
4. Dip each doughnut into the glaze. Twist the doughnut as you remove it from the glaze to give it a nice finish and prevent dripping.

Chef's tips

When pouring the hot cream into the sugar syrup, the caramel is highly bubbling. Therefore, it is best to use a deep saucepan, for safety.

Jam Doughnuts

Are doughnuts an authentic traditional English sweet? I'm not sure, but they are so popular and yummy. They are definitely an English treat!

All types of jam could be heavenly: seedless raspberry jam of course, but why not try a gooseberry, a fig or a rose jam?

🍽 24 Pieces - 30g each

⏱ 20 Minutes preparation time

⏱ 2 Hours 20 minutes to prove

DOUGHNUT DOUGH

- 220g plain flour
- 4 tsp dry yeast
- 240g lukewarm water
- 1 tbsp caster sugar
- 220g strong white flour
- 60g melted vegan spread
- 1tsp baking powder
- 1tsp salt

METHOD

1. Pour half of the lukewarm water, the dry yeast and 1 tbsp caster sugar into the bowl of a mixer with a beater paddle. Mix on a medium speed for 2 minutes or until the dough starts coming away from the sides and forms a ball. Turn off the mixer, cover the dough with a tea towel and let it rest for about 20 minutes.

2. Start the mixer up again on a medium speed and slowly add the melted spread and the remaining 120g water. Once it is all incorporated add the strong white flour, baking powder and salt. Using the hook attachment mix on high speed for 5 minutes until the dough is glossy, smooth and elastic.

3. Cover the bowl with cling film or a clean tea towel and leave to prove at room temperature until it has doubled in size — about 1 hour.

4. Transfer the dough onto a slightly floured worktop. Knock the dough back and roll it into a sausage shape. Cut it into 30g pieces and roll them into smooth tight buns. Place them on a floured baking tray. Cover with a tea towel and leave for about 1 hour, until doubled in size.

5. Fill your deep-fat fryer or heavy-based saucepan halfway with oil. Heat the oil to 180oC. Rapeseed oil is recommended, as it is one of the only unblended oils that can be heated to a high frying temperature without losing its character, colour or flavour. When the oil is heated, carefully slide the doughnuts from the tray using a floured pastry scraper and put them into the oil. Do 2–3 per batch. Fry for 1 ½ minutes each side until golden brown — they puff up and float, so you may need to gently push them down after about 1 minute to help them colour evenly.

6. Remove the doughnuts from the fryer and place them onto kitchen paper. Toss the doughnuts in a bowl of caster sugar while still warm. Repeat the steps until all the doughnuts are fried, but keep checking the oil temperature is correct. Set aside to cool before filling.

7. To fill the doughnuts, make a hole with a small knife or a nozzle. Fill a piping bag with seedless raspberry jam and pipe into the doughnut until nicely swollen.

8. The doughnuts are best eaten straight away, but will keep in an airtight tin.

Pineapple, Coconut and Chocolate Crumble

Would you recognise the traditional English crumble in this tropical version? Rum, coconut, lime, pineapple and Malibu, all the flavours are here to ensure the success of your Latino party or BBQ, and will remain in your guest's memories for a long time …

🍽 4 Glasses 225 ml
⏱ 25 Minutes preparation time
⏱ 15 Minutes cooking time

CHOCOLATE COCONUT CRUMBLE

- 60g plain flour (or gluten free flour)
- 12g unsweetened vegan cocoa powder
- 50g golden caster sugar
- 30g desiccated coconut
- 65g vegan spread

METHOD

1. Preheat the oven to 190oC/Gas mark 5.
2. Tip the flour, the cocoa powder, the sugar and the coconut into a large bowl. Mix all the dry ingredients together with a spatula.
3. Cut the cold vegan spread into cubes. Rub them in with your fingertips until the mixture looks like moist breadcrumbs. Do not overwork the crumble.
4. Sprinkle the crumble evenly over a pre-lined baking tray and bake for about 10 minutes. To assure the crumble will be evenly baked, roughly turn the crumbs over with a fork and bake for another 5 minutes. Let it cool down.

PINEAPPLE CUBES, LIME AND RUM COMPOTE

- 160g pineapple cubes
- 75g pineapple juice
- 75g pineapple and coconut jam
- 1 tsp white rum
- ½ tsp lime juice

METHOD

1. Cut the flesh of a ripe pineapple into small cubes. Put in a heavy bottom saucepan, add the juice and the jam. Cover with a lid and simmer on a medium heat, for about 20 minutes.
2. Add the lime juice and rum. Remove the lid and reduce the compote, stirring from time to time, until it reaches a syrupy consistency.
3. Let it cool down.

YOGHURT CREAM

- 100g solid creamed coconut
- 60g milk alternative
- 300g vegan plain yoghurt
- 2 tbsp corn syrup
- 6 tbsp Malibu liquor

METHOD

1. In the microwave, melt the solid creamed coconut with the milk alternative for about 20 seconds on medium-high power 500W. Transfer into a mixing bowl and, with the paddle attachment, beat the mixture until it reaches a smooth paste texture. Scrape the sides and the bottom of the bowl
2. Slowly incorporate the yoghurt, and finally the corn syrup and Malibu liquor. Give it a last stir, and let it set for ½ hour at least, in the fridge.

GRILLED PINEAPPLE

1. Turn on the oven grill, 190oC/gas mark 5.
2. Soak the skewers in cold water for ½ hour to prevent them from burning.
3. Cut the pineapple in cubes 2cm and thread 4 pieces onto each skewer.
4. Grill for 4 minutes. on each side until slightly blackened.

ASSEMBLING

1. Pour 40g of crumble into the bottom of each glass, cover with 70g of the pineapple compote. Finish with 100g coconut yoghurt. Decorate with a grilled pineapple skewer.

Basil, Raspberry and Coconut Trifle

I love the basil perfume in a dessert, and the basil infusion is a great way to give a cream a floral scent. The marriage with coconut and raspberries and the light fruity taste of the banana sponge transports us on a surprising exotic journey.

🍽 4 Glasses 250ml

⏱ 40 Minutes preparation time

⏱ 15 Minutes cooking time

BASIL PANNA COTTA

- ¾ bunch fresh basil
- 180g oat cream
- 75g milk alternative
- 60g golden caster sugar
- 1 tsp agar agar powder or 1 tbsp agar flakes
- Optional: vegan friendly green food colouring

METHOD

1. Bring the cream to the boil. Turn off the heat. Add the basil into the cream, cover the saucepan with cling film and let the mix infuse — ideally overnight — or for at least 30 minutes. Discard the basil.
2. Dissolve the agar agar in the milk. Bring to the boil, stirring continuously and keep it boiling for about 20 seconds. Meanwhile, in a saucepan, heat up the sugar, lime zests and cream, incorporate the agar agar mix and give it a last boil. Keep aside.

COCONUT WHIPPED CREAM

- 1 can full fat coconut milk (at least 52% coconut fat)
- 2 tbsp maple syrup (or corn, or agave syrup)
- 1 tbsp vanilla extract

METHOD

1. Prepare the coconut whipped cream as explained in the Basics.

VANILLA SPONGE

- 35g plain flour (or gluten free)
- 30g unrefined caster sugar
- 25g ripe banana
- ¼ tsp baking powder
- ¼ tsp baking soda
- 12g milk alternative
- 12g rapeseed oil
- 1 tsp vanilla essence
- 2 tbsp milk alternative

METHOD

1. Prepare a vanilla sponge as explained in the Basics.
2. Line a tray 19 x 13 cm with parchment paper. Pour in the sponge mix and spread evenly with a spatula, 1 ½ cm thick.
3. Bake at 175oC for about 15 minutes. Check if a toothpick inserted in the centre comes out clean. Allow to cool down.

ASSEMBLING

- 250g fresh raspberries
- 6 tbsp raspberry jam
- 50g coconut flakes

METHOD

1. Build up the dessert by alternating the various elements. Start with 25g whipped cream, then about 30g basil panna cotta, then a sponge layer. Repeat these steps and finish with a layer of basil panna cotta. Let the trifle systematically set in the fridge before adding the next level.
2. Display the fresh raspberries on top of the basil panna cotta. Warm up the raspberry jam in the microwave. Eventually add 1 or 2 tbsp of water and gently pour over the fruits. Decorate with coconut flakes.

Pear and Chestnut Crumble

Crumbles are often soggy. This is why I suggest baking the crumble separately. You can even prepare it in advance and keep in an airtight box. Pear and chestnut will warm you up on a cold winter day, and a hint of whisky in the chestnut sauce wouldn't do any harm...

🍽 2 People

⏲ 20 Minutes preparation time

⏲ 15 Minutes cooking time

CRUMBLE

- 50g plain flour (or gluten free flour)
- 10g ground almonds
- 50g demerara sugar
- 50g hard vegan spread

METHOD

1. Preheat the oven to 190oC/Gas mark 5.
2. Tip the flour, the sugar and ground almonds into a large bowl. Mix all the dry ingredients together with a spatula.
3. Cut the cold vegan spread into cubes. Rub them in with your fingertips until the mixture looks like moist breadcrumbs. Do not overwork the crumble.
4. Sprinkle the crumble evenly over a pre-lined baking tray and bake for about 10 minutes. To ensure the crumble will be evenly baked, roughly turn the crumbs over with a fork and bake for another 5 minutes. Let it cool down.

CHESTNUT SAUCE

- 100g vanilla sauce (see Basics)
- 30g sweet chestnut spread
- Optional: a hint of whisky

METHOD

1. Prepare a vanilla sauce as explained in the Basics. In a bowl, whisk together the vanilla sauce, chestnut spread and whisky if you choose to. Eventually, pass through a sieve.

ASSEMBLING

1. Pour the chestnut sauce into the bottom of a pasta or soup bowl. Place a round cutter 8 cm diameter. in the centre and fill with some crumble mix. Remove the cutter and decorate the plate all around with half baby pears and whole chestnuts. Sprinkle some cut rosemary on top of the crumble.

Sushees, Revisited Rice Pudding

This is one of the amazing surprises in this book. A trip into the Far East, or how a savoury icon becomes a sweet treat.

I invented the word "Sushee", it is the combination of sushi and sweets. Although unusual in rice pudding recipes, I love the jasmine rice for its delicate flavour and perfume.

🍴 10 Pieces

⏱ 20 Minutes preparation time

RICE PUDDING

- 40g jasmine rice
- 250g milk alternative
- 125g oat cream
- 50g caster sugar
- ½ vanilla pod
- 20g agar agar mix

METHOD

1. Put the rice, sugar, milk and cream into a heavy bottom, medium sized saucepan. Split the ½ vanilla pod horizontally and scrape the seeds into the pan. Stir and bring to the boil. Reduce the heat. Half cover with a lid, gently cook for 40–45 minutes over a very low heat, stirring occasionally until the rice has swollen and is very tender.
2. Melt the agar agar mix in the microwave, incorporate into the rice and give it a stir.
3. Leave to cool down, ideally overnight in the fridge.

ASSEMBLING

- A few NORI sheets
- Fresh fruits: kiwis, apricots, pineapple…
- Fruit jellies

METHOD

1. Cut the NORI sheets into long stripes, 5 cm wide. With a palette knife, spread the rice onto half of the sheet. Place a fruit or jelly in the middle, same width as the sheet. Make sure the edges are clean and regular. Roll the sheet into a sushi shape.
2. Store them in the fridge before serving.

Elderflower, Rosè Wine and Fruit Jelly

I love the sweet and delicate flavour of elderflower and it is a perfect match with the fruits in this colourful dessert. The sparkling rosé wine will add some pep to this mouth-watering jelly.

🍽 4 Glasses 150ml

⏱ 20 Minutes preparation time

JELLY

- 120g vegan sparkling rosé wine or champagne
- 150g elderflower cordial
- 85g sugar syrup
- 120g water
- 2 tbsp agar flakes or 2 tsp agar powder
- 400g assorted fruits

METHOD

1. Firstly, prepare the syrup by boiling 75g of water with 40g unrefined caster. Keep aside.
2. Dissolve the agar agar in the water and bring to the boil, whisking constantly. Keep it boiling for about 20 seconds.
3. Meanwhile, warm up all the remaining liquids. Add the agar agar mix.
4. Cut the fruits into small cubes or balls. Preferably, choose firm fruits such as blueberries, red currants, apricots, grapes…
5. Pour a thin layer (1cm) of jelly into the bottom of the glass. Let it set for 20 minutes in the fridge. Put one layer of fruits on top of it and cover with jelly. Bring back to the fridge. Repeat this operation 2–3 times until it reaches the top of the glass.
6. Keep the glasses in the fridge. Decorate with a skewer of fresh fruits. Serve at room temperature.

Chef's tips

If you want to prepare the jelly in advance, it can be kept in the freezer. Just defrost it in the microwave.

Tarts, Cakes and Gateaux

Black Forest Gateau

You will find various adaptations of this cake, which originated from Germany. Respecting the traditional components — cherries, cream and sponge — I introduced an exquisite chocolate mousse to enrich the balance and interest of the flavours. The kirsch liquor made from cherries will gently excite your palate. Now time for tasting!

🍽 6 Cakes 6cm height, 7cm diameter

⏱ 40 Minutes preparation time

⏱ 20 Minutes cooking time

CHOCOLATE SPONGE

- 150g golden caster sugar
- 130g self-raising flour
- 20g unsweetened vegan cocoa powder
- 1 tsp baking powder
- 50g rapeseed oil
- 150g water

METHOD

1. Prepare a chocolate sponge as explained in the Basics.
2. Pour the sponge into a pre-lined baking tray and bake at 175oC/ gas mark 4, for 20 minutes. Let it cool down.
3. Cut 12 circles, same size as the rings. Keep aside.

CHOCOLATE MOUSSE

- 220g vegan dark chocolate
- 6 tbsp thick coconut milk (see Basics)
- 1 ripe crushed avocado
- 8 tbsp maple syrup or agave nectar
- 30g oat cream
- 60g reduced aquafaba (see Basics)

METHOD

1. Prepare a chocolate mousse as explained in the Basics.

CHERRY WHIPPED CREAM

- 360g coconut whipped cream
- 6 tsp corn syrup
- 120g agar agar mix (see Basics)
- 3 tsp kirsch
- 100g fresh cherries

METHOD

1. 1. Prepare a coconut whipped cream as explained in the Basics.
2. 2. Cut the cherries into small pieces.
3. 3. Melt the agar agar mix in the microwave. Add the kirsch liquor and gently incorporate to the whipped cream with a spatula. Finally fold in the pieces of cherries.

ASSEMBLING

1. Place your rings onto parchment paper. They will be easier to transfer to a plate.
2. In the bottom of each ring, start with a layer of chocolate sponge, then pipe about 70g of chocolate mousse on top of the sponge. Press with a second sponge layer, and finish with the cherry cream and flatten with a palette knife. Transfer to the freezer for ½ hour at least.
3. Remove the cakes from the mould. With a sharp knife scrape some chocolate flakes from a chocolate bar. Sprinkle over the cake. Pipe a dot of whipped cream using a star nozzle, 10mm diameter. Dust some icing sugar on and finish with a cherry on top.

Raspberry Mille-Feuilles

It is really worth giving this homemade puff pastry a try! It won't compare with the "Jus Roll" brands which contain a lot of odd ingredients, including palm oil!

🍴 4   Pieces 7 x 7 cm

⏱ 1   Hour preparation time

⏱ 18-20 Minutes cooking time

PUFF PASTRY

- 200g extra strong flour
- 4g salt
- 20g vegan spread
- +/- 120g water
- 170g hard vegan spread

METHOD

1. Prepare a puff pastry as explained in the Basics.
2. On a lightly floured worktop, roll out the pastry 3–4 mm thick. Cut a rectangle 30 x 15 cm. Divide into 8 pieces 7.5 x 7.5 cm. Transfer to a pre-lined baking tray or silicone mat, leaving at least 1cm space between each piece. Brush with some alternative milk and soft brown sugar to give a golden colour.
3. Let them rest ½ hour before baking.
4. Preheat the oven to 200oC/gas mark 5 and bake for 18–20 minutes.

LIGHT CUSTARD CREAM

- 125g milk alternative (koko, rice, soya …)
- 25g golden caster sugar
- 15g cornflour
- ½ tsp cashew butter
- a few drops of vanilla essence
- 10g vegan spread
- vegan friendly yellow colouring (optional)
- 60g coconut whipped cream (see Basics)
- 20g agar agar mix (see Basics)
- 1 punnet raspberries

METHOD

1. Prepare a custard as explained in the Basics.
2. Keep refrigerated.
3. With a spatula, gently fold the whipped cream into the custard. Bring back to the fridge.

ASSEMBLING

1. Pour the cream into a piping bag, plain nozzle 4mm diameter. Place some raspberries — same size — at the edges of a puff pastry square. Fix them with some dots of light cream. Pipe some cream in the middle to allow the 2nd puff pastry square to stick. Place the golden caramel square on top.

Chef's tips

If you want to give a golden caramel colour to your mille-feuilles, just sprinkle the 4 top squares with icing sugar, bring the oven temperature to 225oC/gas mark 6 and leave them for 1–2 minutes. Careful, they burn very easily! In summer, it might be wise to add some agar agar mix to the cream: Dissolve 20g of the mix, pour into the cream and give it a quick whisk.

Apricot, Vanilla Panna Cotta and French Sablè

There are no words to describe this elegant, exquisite little jewel! If you enjoy a light custard you should try this Italian panna cotta. Its fine wobble texture contrasts with the crispy French sablé pastry. The edible flower should be the pearl on the cake…

Perfectly freezable, you can play with funny little moulds.

🍽 8 Drops 7.5cm x 3,5cm height
⏱ 30 Minutes preparation time
⏱ 15 Minutes cooking time

VANILLA PANNA COTTA

- 1 ½ tsp agar agar powder or 1 ½ tbsp agar flakes
- 75g milk alternative
- 190g oat cream
- 85g golden caster sugar
- 1 vanilla pod

METHOD

1. Dissolve the agar agar in the milk alternative. Bring to the boil, stirring continuously, keep it boiling for 20 seconds.
2. Cut the vanilla pod in half, length wise, scrape the seeds and pour into the cream.
3. Meanwhile, in a saucepan, heat up the sugar and cream, incorporate the agar agar and milk. Give it a last stir. Pour the panna cotta into the appropriate moulds.
4. Transfer to the freezer for 4 hours at least. Remove the panna cotta from the mould and put on top of the sweet pastry.

FRENCH SABLÉ PASTRY

- 40g vegan spread
- 60g sifted icing sugar
- 20g milk alternative
- 100g plain flour
- ½ tsp. baking powder
- pinch of salt

METHOD

1. Prepare a French sablé pastry as explained in the Basics p--.
2. Preheat the oven to 190oC/gas mark 5.
3. Roll out the pastry between 2 sheets of parchment paper, ½ cm thick. Transfer on a pre-lined baking tray or silicone mat. Slightly grease the inside of a stainless drop. Cut the desired shape, but leave the stainless drop while baking. Bake the pastry for 10 minutes at 190oC. Remove the stainless drop and bake for another 5 minutes. With this technique, the pastry edges will remain clean, straight and regular.

ASSEMBLING

1. Remove the panna cottas from the mould and place on top of the sablé pastry bases.
2. Decorate with a slice of fresh apricot, some rosemary and edible flowers.

Iced Strawberry Soufflè with a Sesame Shortbread

This is a wonderfully easy dessert to make! You can of course prepare it in advance and get it out of the freezer as soon as the sunshine is out! Most fruits are suitable for this recipe, you can even combine two different fruits and marble the soufflé!

🍴 6 Ramequins 8cm diameter x 5cm deep
⏱ 30 Minutes preparation time
⏱ 12 Minutes cooking time

STRAWBERRY COMPOTE

- 375g strawberries
- 90g unrefined caster sugar
- ½ tsp lemon juice

METHOD

1. Cut the strawberries in half or into quarters if large, and put in a heavy bottom saucepan with the sugar and lemon juice. Heat gently and stir until the sugar dissolves, then bring to a simmer. Cook the strawberries for 10–12 minutes until dark red and syrupy. Allow to cool down.

STRAWBERRY SOUFFLÉ MIX

- 6 x 125g vegan strawberry yoghurt
- 120g coconut whipped cream
- 150g reduced aquafaba (see Basics)
- 360g strawberry compote

METHOD

1. Prepare 6 individual soufflé dishes: Spray a strong double layer of greaseproof paper (3 cm x 23cm) with rapeseed oil. Tie around the edge to form a collar that stands 1 ½ cm above the rim. Secure with tape. Transfer to the freezer for ½ hour at least.

2. In the meantime, in a mixing bowl, using the paddle attachment, gently stir together the yoghurt, coconut cream and strawberry compote. Put the aquafaba into a perfectly clean bowl. With an electric hand mixer, whisk the aquafaba until it forms stiff peaks. Delicately fold the meringue into the fruit yoghurt mix, then spoon into the prepared soufflé dishes. Freeze for 12 hours.

3. Remove from the freezer ½ hour before serving. Delicately slip a spatula around the paper collar and remove the paper. Decorate with fresh strawberries.

SESAME SHORTBREAD

- 50g unrefined caster sugar
- 110g vegan spread
- 150g plain flour (or gluten free flour)
- 2 pinches of salt
- 2tbsp roasted sesame seeds

METHOD

1. Preheat the oven 190oC/gas mark 5.
2. Prepare a shortbread pastry as explained in the Basics. Wrap in cling film and let it rest for 2hours at least in the fridge.
3. Roll out about 8mm thick between 2 sheets of parchment paper. Lift the bottom paper onto a baking tray. Cut long sharp shapes (oriental sticks) with a knife. Sprinkle with the roasted sesame seeds and bake for about 12 minutes at 190oC/gas mark 5.

Le Fraisier – Classical French Strawberry Cake

I propose to re-baptise it "the Wimbledon cake"!

This is a brilliant answer of how to combine creamy, fruity, soft and crispy textures, all at the same time!

🍽 6 Cakes 8cm diameter, 3,5cm height
⏱ 30 Minutes preparation time
⏱ 15 Minutes + 15 minutes cooking time

FRENCH SABLÉ PASTRY

- 50g vegan spread
- 75g sifted icing sugar
- 25g milk alternative
- 125g plain flour
- ¼ tsp. baking powder
- pinch of salt

METHOD

1. Prepare a French sablé pastry as explained in the Basics.
2. Preheat the oven to 190oC/gas mark 5.
3. On a lightly floured worktop, roll out the pastry between 2 sheets of parchment paper, 2mm thick. Cut 6 circles same size as the rings and transfer onto a pre-lined baking tray or a silicone mat. Bake for 15 minutes at 190oC.

MOUSSELINE CREAM

- 250g milk alternative
- 1 tbsp cashew butter
- 25g cornflour
- ½ vanilla pod
- 50g unrefined caster sugar
- 80g hard vegan spread
- 250g fresh strawberries medium size

METHOD

1. Prepare a custard as explained in the Basics
2. Allow to cool down.
3. Soften the vegan spread in the microwave for 10 seconds. Transfer to a mixing bowl. Using the whisk attachment, at medium speed, slowly add the custard- about ¼ at a time -making sure the cream remains smooth. Scrape the bowl 1–2 times. Keep refrigerated.

VICTORIA SPONGE

- 75g self-raising flour
- 45g unrefined caster sugar
- ¼ tsp baking powder
- 75g milk alternative
- 30g rapeseed oil
- 1 tsp vanilla essence

METHOD

1. Preheat the oven 190oC/gas mark 5.
2. Prepare a sponge as explained in the Basics. Pour into a pre-lined baking tray 19 x 13 cm. Bake for 15 minutes at 190oC.Let it cool down.

ASSEMBLING

1. Place the sweet pastry disc in the bottom of a stainless ring. Cut the strawberries in half, flat side against the ring. Strawberries should be the same size.

2. With a piping bag cover the pastry base with a layer of mousseline cream, about 30g. Make sure you fill the spaces between the half strawberries. With a round cutter, cut 6 discs about 3cm diameter in the sponge and place on top of the mousseline. Fill the ring with the remaining cream to the top. Flatten with a palette knife. Let it set in the fridge for 3 hours at least.

3. Remove the ring. Cover the top of the cake with a red marzipan disc, same size as the ring. Decorate with a strawberry.

Fresh Fruits "Kilometre" Tart

Imagine a huge outdoor wedding party with 10 yards of these kilometre tarts.

🍽 1   Tart 30 x 11cm.

⏱ 1   Hour preparation time

⏱ 18-20 Minutes cooking time

PUFF PASTRY

- 200g extra strong flour
- 4g salt
- 20g vegan spread
- +/- 120g water
- 170g hard vegan spread

METHOD

1. Prepare a puff pastry as explained in the Basics.
2. On a lightly floured worktop, roll out the pastry 3–4 mm thick. Cut out a rectangle 32 x 13cm. Cut 1cm off each long side and place on top of the edges to create a border. Brush with some alternative milk and soft brown sugar to give a golden colour and transfer to a pre-lined baking tray.
3. Let them rest ½ hour before baking. Bake for 18–20 minutes at 200oC/ gas mark 5–6.

CUSTARD

- 250g milk alternative
- 50g caster sugar
- 25g cornflour
- 1 tbsp cashew butter
- a few drops of vanilla essence
- vegan friendly yellow food colouring (optional)

METHOD

1. Prepare a custard as explained in the Basics.
2. With a nozzle 10 diameter. pipe the custard on top of the tart.
3. Garnish with some fresh fruits.
4. Warm up some light apricot marmalade and brush delicately onto the fruits.

Le Vacherin

One impressive-looking cake. Build up with layers of meringue and strawberry mousse, then encase it in meringue sticks... A hit for a summer party!

🍽 12 People springform tin 23cm diameter

⏱ 40 Minutes + extra time to set preparation time

⏱ 1 Hour 15 minutes cooking time

MERINGUE

- 90g reduced aquafaba (see Basics)
- 170g caster sugar

METHOD

1. Peheat the oven to 100oC /gas mark ¼ and line 2 baking trays with parchment paper or a silicone mat. On cardboard, draw and cut out a circle 22cm diameter. Then draw and cut out a rectangle 7 cm high. Place them on the baking trays, under the silicone mat or parchment paper.

2. In a perfctly clean bowl, whisk the reduced aquafaba until it reaches soft peaks. Slowly add the sugar and continue to whisk to stiff peaks.

3. Pour the meringue into a piping bag with a plain nozzle 12mm diameter.

4. Pipe the meringue over the cardboard circle and the sticks over the rectangle cardboard. This way, they will all have the same size.

5. Bake the sticks for about 30–45 minutes and the circles for about 1 hour 15 minutes–1 hour 30 minutes at 100oC.

6. Let the meringue rest at room temperature for 10 minutes before removing from the mats.

STRAWBERRY PUREE

- 250g frozen strawberries
- 50g unrefined caster sugar

METHOD

1. Bring the strawberries and sugar to the boil, let them simmer for a few minutes and purée the fruits in a blender.
2. Keep refrigerated.

STRAWBERRY MOUSSE

- 1kg strawberry purée
- 4 tsp agar agar powder or 4 tbsp agar flakes
- 3–4 tbsp golden caster sugar (depending on the sweetness of the fruit)
- 650g silken tofu

METHOD

1. Prepare a strawberry mousse as explained in the Basics (fruit mousse)

ASSEMBLING

- 2 punnets of assorted red fruits (strawberries, raspberries, pomegranate…)

METHOD

1. Place the first meringue circle in the bottom of the springform tin. Cover with half of the strawberry mousse. Let it set at room temperature for ½ hour.
2. Repeat these steps and transfer the cake to the freezer for ½ hour at least
3. Remove the cake from the mould and place on a plate. Let it defrost for 20 minutes at least before you start to fix the meringue sticks all around the cake.
4. Decorate with the fruits.

Opèra Cake

This cake is a great thing to have in your repertoire. Pistachio, passionfruit and raspberry make a mosaic of soft, warm colours, like summertime.

🍽 5 Cakes 3 x 8 cm
⏱ 40 Minutes preparation time
⏱ 15 Minutes cooking time
⏱ 2 Hours to set

- 25g ground almonds
- 25g ground pistachios
- 25g plain flour
- ¼ tsp baking soda
- 15g cornflour
- 40g golden caster sugar
- 65g milk alternative
- 1 ½ tbsp rapeseed oil

METHOD

1. Prepare a pistachio sponge as explained in the Basics.
2. Pour the sponge into a pre-lined baking tray 20 x 25 cm. Spread evenly with a palette knife and bake at 190oC for 15 minutes.

PASSION FRUIT MOUSSELINE

- 125g passion fruit juice or purée
- 30g golden caster sugar
- 15g cornflour
- ½ tbsp cashew butter
- 50g vegan spread

METHOD

1. In a mixer whisk together the cashew butter, sugar, cornflour and about 25 ml of the liquid. Meanwhile, in a heavy bottom saucepan, bring the remaining juice to the boil. Remove from the heat, pour the previous mix into the boiling liquid, continue to whisk until all the ingredients are evenly combined. Bring back to a low heat and stir continuously until the mixture starts bubbling and thickens. Transfer to the fridge.
2. Soften the vegan spread in the microwave for 10 seconds. Slowly add the passion fruit cream and, with an electric hand mixer, whisk until fluffy.
3. Keep refrigerated.

RASPBERRY JELLY

*   125g raspberry purée
*   30g golden caster sugar
*   ¾ tsp agar agar powder or ¾ tbsp agar flakes.

METHOD

1. 1. In a heavy bottom saucepan, bring all the ingredients to the boil, stirring continuously.
2. 2. When the jelly reaches boiling point, continue to whisk for another 20 seconds, then take off the heat. Allow to cool.

ASSEMBLING

1. The refinement of this cake resides in its apparent simplicity, for it is important the layers are regular and neat. Therefore, I suggest to assemble the cake in these individual rectangle moulds.
2. Cut 10 pistachio sponges 3 x 8 cm. Place the first one in the bottom of the mould. Pipe a layer of passion fruit mousseline (about 3 mm thick) on top of the sponge and let it set for ½ hour at least, in the freezer.
3. Melt the jelly gently in the microwave 15 seconds at a time. The temperature should not exceed 45oC. Pour over the passion fruit cream, same thickness. Return to the freezer for another ½ hour.
4. Repeat these steps a second time and let the cake set in the freezer.
5. Meanwhile, temper 150g of vegan alternative white chocolate as explained in the Basics. Cut 10 triangles, same length as the cake. Stick on each side of the cake and finish with a golden leaf.

Mini Cakes & Petits Fours

Blueberry and Coconut Cupcakes

Whether it's their tiny size, their pretty decoration or the memories of childhood, cupcakes really do have ultimate treat appeal. Their declinations are infinite and suitable for all seasons and occasions. This recipe is great for lazy summer days, when plump and juicy blueberries are at the height of the season.

🍴 12 Pieces

⏱ 20 Minutes preparation time

⏱ 25 Minutes cooking time

COCONUT CUPCAKE

- 215g golden caster sugar
- 110g plain flour
- 100g desiccated coconut
- 3 tsp baking powder
- 1 tsp baking soda
- 1 tsp apple cider vinegar
- 130g milk alternative

METHOD

1. Preheat the oven to 165oC/ gas mark 3.
2. Line a 12-piece muffin pan with muffin paper cases.
3. Sift the flour, baking powder and baking soda. Using the paddle attachment, mix all the dry ingredients together at low speed. Add the vinegar and milk alternative. Beat the mix at medium speed until it's a smooth consistency, with no remaining lumps.
4. With a spoon or a piping bag, divide the cupcake mix evenly among the 12 paper cases, fill about 4/5, allowing the cupcakes to rise.
5. Bake for about 25 minutes, or until a toothpick inserted into the centre comes out clean.

BLUEBERRY FROSTING

- 400g hard vegan cream cheese
- 100g blueberry jam

METHOD

1. In a mixing bowl, using the paddle, beat together the cream cheese and blueberry jam to make a light, fluffy icing.
2. Pour the frosting into a piping bag, using a star nozzle 12mm diameter. Pipe onto the cakes. At this stage, the cupcakes can be kept in the freezer. Decorate with a few blueberries.

Chef's tips

After baking, the colour of the cupcake will remain quite light. This is due to the lack of eggs. If you want the cupcakes to get a golden colour, just place them for 1 minute under the grill.

Valentine's Cupcakes

This adorable little cupcake will be ideal for a glamourous Valentine's treat. They can be made in advance, just take 5 minutes to decorate, and will leave you plenty of time to enjoy a wonderful romantic day.

For the recipe refer to the "Blueberry cupcake ", just replace the blueberry jam by strawberry.

DECORATION

1. Gently peel off the skin of the strawberries and cut them into slices.
2. Using a tiny heart cutter, cut a little heart shape in each slice, and decorate the cupcake delicately.

Chef's tips

For your first step in confectionary, this recipe is incredibly easy, all you need is an accurate thermometer… and a wooden spoon!

Strawberry Pate De Fruits

For your first step in confectionary, this recipe is incredibly easy, all you need is an accurate thermometer… and a wooden spoon!

🍽 1 Tray 19 cm x 13 cm
⏱ 20 Minutes preparation time

Strawberry Pate De Fruits

- 250g strawberry purée
- 75g glucose
- 250g golden caster sugar (200+50)
- 17g pectin
- an extra 150g caster sugar

METHOD

1. Pre-line a baking tray 19 x 13 cm with double cling film.
2. Cook the strawberry purée, glucose and 200g sugar in a heavy bottom saucepan, on a medium heat. Give it a few stirs to avoid the sugar sticking to the bottom of the saucepan, until the temperature reaches 102oC.
3. Mix together the pectin and the remaining 50g sugar. Pour into the strawberry mix, and stir continuously until the temperature reaches 108oC.
4. Pour the pate de fruits into the baking tray. Let it set at room temperature. Cut little cubes 2cm and roll them in the caster sugar.

Mango and Passion Fruit Marshmallows

Making your own marshmallows is a fun affair! Soft, fluffy, chewy, pillowy…They will disappear in less time than it takes to count 1,2,3! Most kind of fruits are suitable for this recipe.

🍴 24 Pieces 3 x 3 x 3cm

⏱ 20 Minutes preparation time

MANGO AND PASSION FRUIT MARSHMALLOWS

- 125g caster sugar
- 40g water
- 1tsp agar agar powder or 1 tbsp agar flakes
- 40g reduced aquafaba (see Basics)
- 125g mango and passion fruit juice
- 75g icing sugar + 75g cornflour

METHOD

1. Tip the reduced aquafaba into a perfectly clean mixing bowl.
2. Prepare an Italian meringue : Pour the sugar and water into a heavy bottom saucepan and gently cook the sugar syrup at medium heat. When the temperature reaches 110oC, start to whisk the aquafaba in a mixing bowl at high speed, until it comes to stiff peaks. When the temperature reaches 118oC, reduce the speed to medium level and slowly add the sugar syrup to the aquafaba. When all the syrup is incorporated, bring the meringue to high speed again, and whisk until it has cooled down.
3. In the meantime, dissolve the agar agar powder or flakes in the fruit juice. Bring to the boil, stirring continuously. Keep it boiling for another 20 seconds.
4. Slowly pour the juice into the meringue, and whisk until smooth and homogeneous consistency.

5. Transfer the marshmallow mix into a prelined tray 13 x19 cm.
6. Let it cool down at room temperature.
7. When the mix is set, cut into cubes 3 x 3 x 3cm and roll each piece in a mix of ½ icing sugar + ½ cornflour.

Pineapple Marshmallows

Although marshmallows might have a childish connotation, this flower display will have a sensational effect on your buffets!

🍽 24 Pieces
⏱ 30 Minutes preparation time

PINEAPPLE MARSHMALLOWS

- 125g caster sugar
- 40gl water
- 1tsp agar agar powder or 1tbsp agar flakes
- 40g reduced aquafaba (see Basics)
- 125g pineapple juice juice
- 75g icing sugar + 75g cornflour

METHOD

1. Prepare a marshmallow mix as explained in the previous recipe, just replace the mango and passion fruit juice with pineapple.
2. When the mix is set, cut into a flower shape and roll in a mix of ½ icing sugar and ½ cornflour.

PRESENTATION

1. Cut off the bottom of a fresh pineappple.
2. Place each marshmallow onto a toothpick and display all around the pineapple.

Chef's tips

If you want to add a delicate little detail, you can pipe a pink dot on the flower. It is just some icing sugar with vegan spread, and a trace of pink food colouring. But it makes the whole difference!

Mini Madeleines

These little French sponge cakes are traditionally baked in shell shaped moulds.

The light citrus flavour will add a tangy and refreshing touch. Perfect to accompany a 5 o'clock tea or coffee.

🍴 24 Pieces
⏱ 10 Minutes preparation time
⏱ 7-8 Minutes cooking time

Mini Madeleines

- 1 ¼ tsp flaxseeds mix
- 40g vegan spread
- 40g icing sugar
- 20g milk alternative
- 50g self-raising flour
- ½ tsp baking powder
- ½ lime or lemon zest

METHOD

1. Firstly, prepare the flaxseeds mix: Mix 10g of flaxseeds with 30ml of cold water and let it set in the fridge for 15 minutes at least.
2. Preheat the oven to 225oC/gas mark 6.
3. Melt the vegan spread in the microwave.
4. In the meantime, place all the ingredients into a mixing bowl, except the vegan spread.
5. Using the paddle, gently beat the mix at medium speed. Add the melted spread and give it a last stir.
6. Fill up the mini madeleines moulds with a spoon or piping bag.
7. Bake at 225oC for 5 minutes, and another 2–3 minutes at 200oC.

Lemon and Poppy Seeds Kisses

The name of this petit four is inspired by the French "Baisers de dames", "Ladies kisses". This is not even a specific recipe: If you have some left over meringue from your Eton Mess or Vacherin, just add some poppy seeds and a few drops of Sicilian lemon essence, done!

🍽 30 Pieces

⏱ 30 Minutes preparation time

⏱ 30-40 Minutes cooking time

LEMON AND POPPY SEEDS MERINGUE

- 100g left over meringue
- a few drops Sicilian lemon essence
- 2 tbsp poppy seeds
- vegan friendly yellow food colouring

METHOD

- 100g left over meringue
- a few drops Sicilian lemon essence
- 2 tbsp poppy seeds
- vegan friendly yellow food colouring

LEMON MOUSSELINE

- 125g milk alternative
- 25g golden caster sugar
- 12g cornflour
- ½ tsp cashew butter
- zest of an organic lemon
- 50g hard vegan spread
- vegan friendly yellow food colouring

METHOD

1. Prepare a custard as explained in the Basics. Allow to cool down.
2. Soften the vegan spread in the microwave for 10 seconds. Transfer to a bowl. With an electric hand whisk, slowly add the custard and beat until smooth.
3. Keep refrigerated.

ASSEMBLING

- 200g vegan dark chocolate

METHOD

1. Temper the dark chocolate as explained in the Basics.
2. Dip the bottom of each meringue in the chocolate and let it set on a rack at room temperature.
3. With a star nozzle, pipe some mousseline on top of half the meringues. Cover with the second half.

Chef's tips

If you want to add a delicate little detail, you can pipe a pink dot on the flower. It is just some icing sugar with vegan spread, and a trace of pink food colouring. But it makes the whole difference!

Festive Desserts

Christmas Boot

In this last chapter, we look at a world of magic, dreams and fantasy, where the boots walk, the trees talk and the birds fly!

🍽 1 Boot 30 x 24 cm

⏱ 40 Minutes preparation time

⏱ 20 Minutes cooking time

CHOCOLATE BROWNIE

- 315g plain flour
- 300g golden caster sugar
- 65g unsweetened vegan cocoa powder
- 250g mashed ripe banana
- ½ tbsp baking powder
- ½ tbsp bicarbonate of soda
- 115g milk alternative
- 115g rapeseed oil

METHOD

1. Preheat the oven 190o C/gas mark 5.
2. Whizz all the ingredients in a food processor until the brownie mix becomes smooth and homogeneous, with no remaining lumps.
3. Pour the brownie mix into a pre-lined baking tray 30 x 24 cm. Evenly spread with a palette knife — 2cm thick — and bake at 190°C for 18–20 minutes. Check if a toothpick inserted in the centre comes out clean. Allow to cool down.

HOMEMADE MARZIPAN

- 250g ground almonds
- 250g icing sugar
- 80g water
- 1 tsp lemon juice
- Optional: ½ tsp rose water
- vegan friendly red food colouring

METHOD

1. Whizz all the ingredients — except the colouring — together in a food processor. Keep 100g natural marzipan and mix the remaining marzipan with the red food colouring. Cling film both separately.

ASSEMBLING

1. On cardboard, draw and cut a boot shape. Place on top of the brownie and cut, following the shape.
2. Slightly dust your work surface with sifted icing sugar. Roll out the red marzipan, making sure the surface will cover 4/5 of the boot. Carefully transfer onto the brownie, cut the paste along the edges. Similarly roll out the white marzipan and cut into a rectangle 6cm x 25cm.Fold in half horizontally, transfer to the boot and place on top of the red paste, as the picture shows. Cut the edges.
3. Decorate with fancy, colourful little things (chocolate truffles, coconut flakes, marzipan gift boxes, Christmas decors...)

Mulled Cider and Apple Trifle

Although this dessert might look quite sophisticated and time consuming, you shouldn't feel worried, as most of the components for this recipe can be prepared in advance. Having said so, this dessert celebrates a very special occasion and it's definitely worth spending some time on it!

🍽 2 Glasses 500ml

⏱ 45 Minutes preparation time

⏱ 10 Minutes cooking time

SPICY MULLED CIDER JELLY

- 100g apple juice
- 250g dry cider
- 2 tbsp orange juice
- 1 ½ tsp agar agar powder or 1 ½ tbsp agar flakes
- 2 tbsp soft brown sugar
- 40g golden caster sugar
- ½ cinnamon stick
- 1 clove
- 2 star anis

METHOD

1. Dissolve the agar agar in the liquids (apple juice, dry cider and orange juice) and gently bring them to the boil, whisking continuously. Keep it boiling for another 20 seconds. Add the spices and sugars and give it a last stir. Take off the heat and let it cool down at room temperature. Before the jelly sets, discard the spices. Pour the jelly into the bottom of the glasses. Transfer to the fridge and let it set for ½ hour.

SPICY CUSTARD

- 375g milk alternative
- 75g unrefined golden caster sugar
- 40g cornflour
- 1 ½ tbsp cashew butter
- 1 tsp ground ginger
- 1 tsp cinnamon
- ½ tsp all spices
- 45g oat cream

METHOD

1. Prepare a custard as explained in the Basics. Incorporate the spices, the cream and allow to cool.

GINGERBREAD BISCUITS

- 90g plain flour
- 1 tsp ginger
- ½ tsp cinnamon
- ½ baking powder
- 30g vegan spread
- 45g soft light sugar
- ½ tbsp rapeseed oil
- 1 tbsp maple syrup
- 1 tbsp milk alternative

METHOD

1. Preheat the oven to 190oC/gas mark 5.
2. In a mixing bowl, using the paddle, beat together the sugar and vegan spread until fluffy. Incorporate all the dry ingredients, then the liquids (oil, maple syrup and milk) and gently mix on a low speed. Do not overwork the pastry.
3. Wrap the pastry with cling film and let it rest in the fridge, ideally overnight, or for 2 hours at least.
4. On a lightly floured work surface, roll out the pastry 3mm thick. Cut some star shapes with a cutter. (This recipe gives about 24 pieces). With a palette knife, transfer to a pre-lined baking tray and bake at 190oC for 10 minutes. Allow to cool down.

ALMOND SPONGE

- 100g ground almonds
- 60g plain flour (or gluten free flour)
- ½ tsp soda
- 50g cornflour
- 2 tbsp flaxseeds mix
- 160g unrefined caster sugar
- 100g milk alternative
- 100g melted vegan spread

METHOD

1. Preheat the oven to 190oC/gas mark 5.
2. Prepare an almond sponge as explained in the Basics. Pour the sponge into a pre-lined baking tray 25 x 30 cm and bake at 190oC for 15 minutes.
3. Allow to cool down and cut 4 discs, the same size as the trifle glass.

APPLE COMPOTE

- 500g fresh apples
- 75g apple juice
- 50g golden caster sugar

METHOD

1. Cut 500g of fresh apples in little cubes and cook them with a splash of apple juice and 50g of golden caster sugar until soft. Mix with 150g of liquid mulled cider jelly.

ASSEMBLING

1. Pour the jelly into the bottom of the glass and transfer to the fridge to set for ½ hour.
2. Place a disc of sponge on top of the jelly, cover with a layer of spicy custard, about 1 ½ cm thick and transfer to the fridge for ½ hour. At this stage, decorate the side of the glasses with the gingerbread biscuits stars.
3. Repeat with a second layer of sponge and custard. Cover with the apple compote. Pour a generous splash of jelly over the compote and let the glasses set in the fridge for ½ hour.
4. Decorate with some star anis, apple balls…

Christmas Chocolate Log

No doubt this decadent chocolate yule log will be the attraction of your Christmas dinner! A moist, rich chocolate sponge is layered with a luxurious chocolate mousse and garnished with fancy homemade Christmas decorations. Not suitable for the faint-hearted!

🍽 1 Log 26 cm long
⏱ 40 Minutes preparation time
⏱ 20 Minutes cooking time

CHOCOLATE SPONGE

- 75g golden caster sugar
- 65g self-raising flour
- 10g unsweetened vegan cocoa powder
- ½ tsp baking powder
- 25g rapeseed oil
- 75g water

METHOD

1. 1. Preheat the oven to 175oC/gas mark 4.
2. 2. Prepare a chocolate sponge as explained in the Basics. Pour the sponge mix into a pre-lined baking tray 22 x 28 cm and bake at 175oC for 20 minutes.

CHOCOLATE MOUSSE

- 220g vegan dark chocolate
- 6 tbsp thick coconut milk (see Basics)
- 1 ripe crushed avocado
- 8 tbsp maple syrup or agave nectar
- 30g oat cream
- 60g reduced aquafaba (see Basics)

METHOD

1.   1. Prepare a chocolate mousse as explained in the Basics.

ASSEMBLING

1.   Slightly grease a yule log mould and line with cling film. Pipe the mousse halfway up the mould. Place a layer of chocolate sponge on top of the mousse, the sponge should be slightly smaller than the mould. Fill the log with the rest of the mousse to the top of the mould and cover with a last layer of chocolate sponge, the same size as the mould.
2.   Transfer to the freezer, let it set for 2 hours at least. Use a warm wet tea towel to remove from the mould.
3.   To give a wooden effect, randomly pass a fork over the cream. Decorate with coconut, homemade marzipan snowmen, dark chocolate, golden leaves, edible Christmas decorations — whatever you fancy.

Chef's tips

If the mousse in getting hard during the building of the cake, just put it in the microwave for a few seconds.

Red Velvet Christmas Tree

A step into the enchanted forest…

🍴 12 Cupcakes
⏲ 30 Minutes preparation time
⏲ 25 Minutes cooking time

RED VELVET CUPCAKE

- 200g self raising flour
- 200g golden caster sugar
- 20g unsweetened vegan cocoa powder
- ¼ tsp baking powder
- ¼ tsp baking soda
- 80g rapeseed oil
- 200g milk alternative
- 4 tsp apple cider vinegar
- 1 tbsp vanilla essence
- vegan friendly red food colouring

METHOD

1. Preheat the oven to 165oC/gas mark 3.
2. Line a 12-piece muffin pan with muffin paper cases.
3. In a mixing bowl, using the paddle attachment, mix all the dry ingredients (flour, sugar, cocoa powder, baking powder and soda) until evenly combined. Pour all the liquids together in a measuring jar (milk alternative, rapeseed oil, cider vinegar and vanilla essence), give them a stir and pour them slowly into the mixing bowl. Finally add the red food colouring. Beat the cupcake mix, medium speed, until it's a smooth consistency, with no remaining lumps.
4. With a spoon or a piping bag, divide the cupcake mix evenly among the 12 paper cases, fill about 4/5, allowing the cupcakes to rise.
5. Bake for about 25 minutes, or until a toothpick inserted into the centre comes out clean.

PISTACHIO PANNA COTTA

- 5 tsp agar agar powder or 5 tbsp agar flakes
- 300g milk alternative
- 750g cream (oat, soya …)
- 240g golden caster sugar
- 1 vanilla pod
- 120g crushed pistachios
- optional: green food colouring

METHOD

1. 1. Dissolve the agar agar in the milk alternative. Bring to the boil, stirring continuously, keep it boiling for 20 seconds.
2. 2. Cut the vanilla pod in half, length wise, scrape the seeds and pour into the milk.
3. 3. Meanwhile, in a saucepan, heat up the sugar and cream, incorporate the agar agar and milk, the crushed pistachios and eventually the food colouring, Pour the panna cotta into the appropriate moulds.
4. 4. Transfer to the freezer for 4 hours at least. Remove the panna cottas from the moulds and put on top of the cupcakes.
5. 5. Decorate with some red marzipan, desiccated coconut and fancy edible Christmas stars.

Easter Chocolate Swan

You may wonder what a swan has to do with Easter... You give up? Well, the body is made with an Easter egg mould! Invite your guests to an Alice in Wonderland journey, where swans walk on a lake or a river!

🍽 6 Pieces 9 cm long, 5 cm deep

⏱ 40 Minutes preparation time

⏱ 15 Minutes cooking time

CHOCOLATE MOUSSE

- 220g vegan dark chocolate
- 30g oat cream
- 8 tbsp thick coconut milk
- 1ripe avocado
- 6 tbsp maple syrup or agave nectar
- 60g reduced aquafaba
- Optional: 2 tbsp hazelnut paste, or matcha powder, coffee extract

METHOD

1. 1. Prepare a chocolate mousse as explained in the Basics.

CHOCOLATE BROWNIE

- 65g plain flour
- 60g unrefined golden caster sugar
- 15g unsweetened vegan cocoa powder
- 50g ripe banana
- ½ tbsp baking powder
- ½ tbsp soda
- 25g milk alternative
- 25g rapeseed oil
- 2 tbsp milk alternative

METHOD

1. Preheat the oven to 190oC/gas mark 5.
2. In a food processor, whizz all ingredients together, except the 2 tbsp milk you will add at the end. The sponge should be slightly runny. Pour the sponge in a pre-lined baking tray 22 x 28 cm, 8mm thick.
3. Bake at 190oC for 15minutes.

ASSEMBLING

1. On cardboard, draw and cut an oval disc, same size as the egg moulds. Cut 6 pieces in the chocolate sponge, keep aside.
2. Fill the egg moulds with the chocolate mousse, using a spoon or a piping bag. Flatten the top with a palette knife. Place the sponges on top of the mousse and transfer to the freezer. Let them set for 4 hours at least.

CHOCOLATE DECORATION

- 150g vegan dark chocolate

METHOD

1. On cardboard, draw and cut 2 wings. Don't forget to make 2 opposite sides, a right and a left one!
2. Temper the dark chocolate as explained in the Basics. With a palette knife, spread the chocolate on an acetate film. Leave it to set at room temperature. Cut the wings just before the chocolate is getting hard.
3. For the heads, pipe the chocolate, using a plain nozzle 5mm diameter, as shown in the picture.
4. Finally, if you really want to surprise your guests, melt some agar agar mix in the microwave. Add some blue colour and delicately pour a thin layer over a plate. Let it set at room temperature and display the swans on top of it.

Lemon Easter Nest

Wrap these nests in a small cellophane bag, and you can hide them in the garden, early in the morning. The kids will be thrilled!

🍴 8 Nests, savarin moulds 6 ½ cm diameter
⏱ 30 Minutes preparation time
⏱ 15 Minutes cooking time

LEMON MOUSSELINE

- 250g milk alternative
- 50g unrefined golden caster sugar
- 25g cornflour
- 1 tbsp cashew butter
- ½ tsp vanilla extract
- Zest of 2 organic lemons
- A few drops Sicilian lemon essence
- 100g hard vegan spread
- vegan friendly yellow food colouring

METHOD

1. Prepare a custard as explained in the Basics. Add the lemon zest and essence.
2. Soften the vegan spread in the microwave for 10 seconds. Transfer to a mixing bowl. Using the whisk attachment, at medium speed, slowly add the custard — about ¼ at a time — making sure the cream remains smooth. Scrape the bowl 1–2 times.
3. Keep refrigerated.

VANILLA SPONGE

- 100g plain flour (or gluten free)
- 90g unrefined golden caster sugar
- 75g ripe banana
- ¾ tsp baking powder
- ¾ tsp soda
- 35g milk alternative
- 35g rapeseed oil
- Zest of 1 organic lemon
- 1 tsp vanilla essence
- 3 tbsp milk alternative

METHOD

1. Preheat the oven to 175oC/gas mark 4.
2. Prepare a vanilla sponge as explained in the Basics. Add the lemon zest. Pour the sponge into a pre-lined baking tray 20 x 29.5 cm. Bake at 175oC for 15minutes.

ASSEMBLING

1. 1. Fill the moulds with the lemon mousseline, using a spoon or a piping bag. Flatten the top with a palette knife.
2. 2. With a round cutter, cut 8 discs 6.5cm diameter in the vanilla sponge. Place on top of the cream and transfer to the freezer. Let them set for 4 hours at least.

DECORATION

VEGAN "BUTTER CREAM"

- 100g vegan spread
- 20g icing sugar
- vegan friendly green food colouring

METHOD

1. 1. Sift the icing sugar. Bring the spread to room temperature. In a mixing bowl, using the paddle, beat all the ingredients together until smooth.

ICING

- 1 tbsp reduced aquafaba (see Basics)
- 80g icing sugar
- ¼ tsp lemon juice or vinegar
- vegan friendly yellow food colouring

METHOD

1. 1. Sift the icing sugar. In a mixing bowl, using the paddle, firmly beat all ingredients together until smooth. Pipe into various shapes: stars, rosettes, pearls… and for the experts, why not try a little bird?

Chef's tips

The vegan "butter cream" should not be overworked, as it might split. If this happens, just warm up the bowl with a blow torch while beating, until the cream recovers its smooth texture.

Sweet Tacos

When the Number 1 Mexican street food turns into sweet... Here are my cute little birds again, and this time, they are bewitched by the scent of rose buds... Yuzu is now becoming increasingly popular. The freshness of a citrussy yuzu mousseline simply announces spring is coming! Or perhaps would you prefer a light chocolate mousse with a drop of rose essence?

🍽 8 Pieces 10 cm diameter

⏱ 30 Minutes preparation time

⏱ 5 Minutes cooking time

CHOCOLATE TUILE MIX

- 30g plain flour
- 5g unsweetened vegan cocoa powder
- 25g icing sugar
- 30g reduced aquafaba (see Basics)
- 25g vegan spread

METHOD

1. Melt the vegan spread in the microwave for 15 seconds on medium power, 350W.
2. With an electric hand mixer, whisk all the ingredients together until smooth. Keep the tuile mix aside.
3. On thin cardboard draw and cut a circle 10cm diameter. Place this template on a silicone mat and spread a thin layer of the tuile mix with a flexible palette knife.
4. To shape the tuile, prepare an angled wooden stick and wrap it in cling film.
5. Preheat the oven to 180oC/gas mark 4.
6. Bake the tuiles for 5 minutes, 1 by 1.
7. Remove the tuile from the mat with a palette knife. Straight away place it around the wooden stick and gently press it with a clean tea towel to give a taco shape.

YUZU MOUSSELINE

- 125g milk alternative
- 125g yuzu juice
- 60g golden caster sugar
- 30g cornflour
- 1½ tbsp cashew butter
- 100g vegan spread

METHOD

1. In a mixer, whisk together the cashew butter, sugar, cornflour and about 50g of the milk alternative. Meanwhile, in a heavy bottom saucepan, bring the remaining milk and juice to the boil. Remove from the heat, pour the previous mix into the boiling liquid, continue to whisk until all the ingredients are evenly combined. Bring back to a low heat and stir continuously until the mixture starts bubbling and thickens. Transfer to the fridge.

2. Soften the vegan spread in the microwave for 10 seconds on medium power, 350W. Slowly add the yuzu cream and, with an electric hand mixer, whisk until fluffy. Store the yuzu mousseline in the fridge.

ASSEMBLING

1.   1. Using a star nozzle 12mm diameter, pipe the mousseline generously inside the tacos and decorate with some green coconut, rose buds, little Easter eggs…

Chef's tips

Your first taco tuile will probably not come out at its best. Don't worry, you will find your way very quickly. If the taco tuile is getting hard before shaping, just briefly reheat it in the oven.

Keep the tuiles in an airtight box.

Basics

Coconut Whipped Cream

- 1 can full fat coconut milk (at least 52% coconut fat)
- 2 tbsp maple syrup (or corn or agave syrup)
- 1 tbsp vanilla extract

METHOD

1. Chill the coconut milk in the fridge overnight.
2. The next day: Place a mixing bowl in the fridge for ½ hour. Open the coconut milk tin, taking care not to shake it. After thorough chilling, the coconut cream will solidify and separate from the milk. Scoop out the solid coconut cream and transfer into the cold mixing bowl (keep the clear milk for further use; smoothies, lollies…). Add the maple syrup and vanilla. Using the paddle attachment, beat the cream until stiff peaks form. For piping work and decorations, use straight away.

Custard

- 250g milk alternative (koko, rice, soya …)
- 50g golden caster sugar
- 25g cornflour
- 1 tbsp cashew butter
- a few drops of vanilla essence
- vegan friendly yellow colouring (optional)

METHOD

1. Pour the milk alternative into a heavy bottom saucepan. Reserve 3 tbsp to be added to the dry ingredients. Bring to the boil.
2. Meanwhile, in a mixer, whisk together the cashew butter, sugar, cornflour, vanilla essence and the reserved liquid. Remove from the heat, pour this mix over the boiling milk and whisk until all the ingredients are evenly combined. Bring back to a low heat and stir continuously until the mixture starts bubbling and thickens. Allow to cool down.

Chef's tips

If you have some remaining cashew butter pieces in your custard, just blend the cream for a few seconds, until smooth. Like all the nuts and seeds butters or oils (tahini, almond butter …), the mix starts to split after a few uses: oil on the top and heavy nut purée at the bottom. You can prevent this by just keeping the jars upside down in your cupboard!

Light Custard

- 120g custard
- 40g coconut whipped cream
- 10g agar agar mix (see Basics)

METHOD

1. Delicately mix both creams with a spatula. In summer you might have to add some agar mix. Melt 10g agar agar mix in the microwave and fold into the light cream. Keep refrigerated.

Mousseline Cream

- 250g milk alternative
- 1 tbsp cashew butter
- 25g cornflour
- a few drops of vanilla essence
- 50g unrefined caster sugar
- 80g hard vegan spread

METHOD

1. Prepare a custard as explained in the Basics. Allow to cool down.
2. Soften the vegan spread in the microwave for 10 seconds on medium power, 350W. Transfer to a mixing bowl. Using the whisk attachment, at medium speed, slowly add the custard — about ¼ at a time — making sure the cream remains smooth. Scrape the bowl 1–2 times. Keep refrigerated.

Vanilla Sauce

- 1 custard recipe
- 100g milk alternative
- 100g oat cream

METHOD

1. Mix all the ingredients together, preferably when the custard is still hot.
2. You can modify the consistency by adapting the amount of liquids.
3. The sauce can be reheated in the microwave 20 seconds at a time on low power, 160W. Avoid boiling.

Chocolate Mousse

- 220g vegan dark chocolate
- 6 tbsp thick coconut milk (see Basics)
- 1 ripe crushed avocado
- 8 tbsp maple syrup or agave nectar
- 30g oat cream
- 60g reduced aquafaba (see Basics)
- Optional: hazelnut paste, coffee extract, matcha powder…

METHOD

1. Melt the chocolate slowly in a microwave, 15 seconds at a time on medium power, 350W (temperature should not exceed 45o degrees). Add the cream and stir until velvety consistency.
2. In a food processor, whizz together the melted chocolate, the coconut milk, the crushed avocado and the syrup. Blend until smooth, making sure the mix doesn't go lumpy.
3. Beat the aquafaba until it forms stiff peaks. Delicately, with a spatula, fold in the chocolate mix. Use straight away.

Fruit Mousses

- 1kg fruit purée
- 4 tsp agar agar powder or 4 tbsp agar flakes
- 3–4 tbsp golden caster sugar (depending on the sweetness of the fruit)
- 650g silken tofu

METHOD

1. Strain the tofu through a muslin. Dissolve the agar agar in the purée and bring to the boil, whisking continuously. Keep it boiling for another 20 seconds. Transfer all the ingredients in a food processor and whizz until smooth and silky consistency.

Chef's tips

Depending on the fruit, you might have to adapt the quantity of agar agar: a passion fruit purée for instance will need up to 6 tbsp.

Choux Pastry

- 125g milk alternative
- 40g vegan spread
- 70g plain flour
- 1 ½ tsp baking powder
- 1 tsp apple cider vinegar
- 3 tbsp vegan egg powder " Follow your heart "
- 180g iced cold water
- 40g reduced aquafaba (see Basics)

METHOD

1. Place 180g water in the freezer. It has to get the iced cold stage.
2. Preheat the oven to 205oC/gas mark 6.
3. In a medium saucepan combine the milk alternative and vegan butter, and slowly bring it to the boil. Reduce to a low heat, add the flour and stir vigorously with a wooden spoon until all the flour is absorbed and forms a homogeneous, silky and dry dough. Transfer to a mixing bowl with the paddle attachment.
4. In a separate bowl, mix the vegan egg powder together with the ice cold water and whisk until it's a smooth consistency. Add the baking powder and the apple cider vinegar.
5. Pour the egg powder mix in the mixing bowl, 1/3 at a time. Beat at high speed, making sure the mix is totally absorbed before adding the next third. Scrape the sides and bottom of the bowl.
6. Finally, slowly add the reduced aquafaba, scrape the bowl one last time and beat until a smooth consistency with no remaining lumps.
7. Pour the choux pastry into a piping bag and bake for 15–20 minutes at 205oC, reduce to 175oC and bake for another15–20 minutes, depending on the size of the choux pastry pieces.

Chocolate Sweet Pastry

- 75g vegan spread
- 100g unrefined golden caster sugar or icing sugar
- 40g milk alternative
- 165g plain flour
- 20g unsweetened vegan cocoa powder
- ¾ tsp baking powder

METHOD

1. In a mixing bowl, using the paddle attachment, beat the vegan spread and the sugar at medium speed, until you reach a fluffy consistency. Reduce the speed and slowly add the milk alternative. Add the flour, the cocoa powder and baking powder. Work on a low speed until all the ingredients are combined. Do not overwork the pastry.
2. Cling film the pastry and allow to rest in the fridge, ideally overnight or for at least 2 hours.

French Sweet Pastry

- 125g plain flour
- ½ tsp. baking powder
- 50g vegan spread
- 75g sifted icing sugar
- 25g milk alternative
- pinch of salt

METHOD

1. In a mixing bowl, using the paddle, at medium speed, beat the spread and the sugar until it's a fluffy consistency. Reduce the speed and incorporate the milk. Add the flour, baking powder and salt. Work on a low speed until all the ingredients are combined. Do not overwork the pastry. Cling film the pastry and allow to rest for at least 2 hours in the fridge.

Puff Pastry

- 200g extra strong flour
- 4g salt
- 20g vegan spread
- +/- 120g water
- 170g hard vegan spread

METHOD

1. In a mixing bowl, using the paddle attachment, mix all the ingredients together at low speed (flour, salt, water and soft vegan spread) for about 30 seconds. Switch to the dough hook, and mix on low speed for +/- 5 minutes, scraping the sides of the mixing bowl if necessary. The dough needs to be smooth and elastic, but not overworked. Transfer to the fridge and let it rest for ½ hour.

2. Roll the dough into a circle. Put the vegan spread in the centre and fold over the right and left sides of the circle, overlapping in the middle. Press the dough with the rolling pin to make it longer and then lightly mark into thirds. Fold the bottom third up to cover the middle third and the top third down. Seal the dough gently by pressing down on the edges with the rolling pin. Give the dough a quarter turn. Repeat 1 more time. Let the pastry rest for at least ½ hour in the fridge.

3. Fold the pastry the same way another 2 times, and put back in the fridge. Let it rest ideally overnight. At this stage, it can be kept in the freezer.

4. Roll out the pastry 3–4 mm thick. Cut out the desired shape and transfer to a pre-lined baking tray.

5. Let it rest ½ hour before baking.

Chef's tips

Depending on the fruit, you might have to adapt the quantity of agar agar: a passion fruit purée for instance will need up to 6 tbsp.

Shortbread

- 50g unrefined caster sugar
- 110g vegan spread
- 150g plain flour
- 2 pinches of salt

METHOD

1. Preheat the oven to 190oC/gas mark 5.
2. In a mixing bowl, using the paddle attachment, at medium speed, beat the vegan spread and sugar until smooth. Tip in the flour and salt. Mix until it's a smooth consistency. Do not overwork the pastry. Wrap in cling film and let it rest for at least 2 hours in the fridge.

Shortcrust Pastry

- 100g vegan spread
- 100g icing sugar
- 70g milk alternative
- 1tsp baking powder
- 200g plain flour

METHOD

1. In a mixing bowl, using a paddle, at medium speed, beat the vegan spread with the icing sugar until it's a fluffy consistency. Reduce the speed and slowly pour the milk alternative. Finish with the baking powder and flour. Do not overwork the pastry.
2. Wrap the pastry in cling film and let it rest in the fridge for at least 1 hour before use.

Almond Sponge

- ½ tbsp flaxseeds mix
- 25g ground almonds
- 15g plain flour
- ¼ tsp baking soda
- 15g cornflour
- 40g unrefined caster sugar
- 2 tbsp milk alternative
- 25g melted vegan spread

METHOD

1. Firstly, prepare the flaxseeds mix: Mix 10g of ground flaxseeds with 30g of cold water and let it rest for at least 15 minutes or until you obtain a thick purée.
2. Preheat the oven to 190oC/ gas mark 4.
3. In a bowl, whisk all the ingredients together. Pour into a pre-lined baking tray, spread evenly — 8mm thick — with a palette knife and bake at 190oC for 15 minutes.
4. Check with a toothpick, that when it is inserted into the centre, it comes out clean. Allow to cool.

Chocolate Sponge

- 75g golden caster sugar
- 65g self-raising flour
- 10g unsweetened vegan cocoa powder
- ½ tsp baking powder
- 25g rapeseed oil
- 75g water

METHOD

1. Preheat the oven 175oC/gas mark 4.
2. In a bowl, whisk all the ingredients together.
3. Pour the sponge mix into a pre-lined baking tray, spread evenly — 8mm thick — with a palette knife and bake at 175oC for 20 minutes.
4. Check with a toothpick, that when it is inserted into the centre, it comes out clean. Allow to cool.

Pistachio Sponge

- 25g ground almonds
- 25g ground pistachios
- 25g plain flour
- ¼ tsp baking soda
- 15g cornflour
- 40g golden caster sugar
- 65g milk alternative
- 1 ½ tbsp rapeseed oil

METHOD

1. Preheat the oven to 190oC/gas mark 5.
2. Grind the pistachios in a food processor.
3. In a mixing bowl, using the paddle attachment, mix all the ingredients together until it's a smooth consistency, with no remaining lumps.
4. Pour the sponge into a pre-lined baking tray. Spread evenly — 8mm thick — with a palette knife and bake at 190oC for 12 minutes.
5. Check with a toothpick, that when it is inserted into the centre, it comes out clean. Allow to cool.

Vanilla Sponge

- 70g plain flour or gluten free flour
- 60g unrefined caster sugar
- 50g ripe banana
- ½ tsp baking powder
- ½ baking soda
- 25g milk alternative
- 25g rapeseed oil
- 1 tsp vanilla essence
- 2 tbsp milk alternative

METHOD

1. Preheat the oven to 175oC /gas mark 4.
2. In a food processor, whizz all the ingredients together, except the 2 tbsp milk alternative you will add at the end. The sponge should be smooth, slightly runny.
3. Pour the sponge into a pre-lined baking tray 22 x 28cm, spread evenly — 1cm thick — with a spatula and bake at 175oC for 15 minutes.
4. Check with a toothpick, that when it is inserted into the centre, it comes out clean. Allow to cool.

Victoria Sponge

- 100g self-raising flour
- 60g unrefined caster sugar
- ½ tsp baking powder
- 100g milk alternative
- 40g rapeseed oil
- 1 tsp vanilla essence

METHOD

1. Preheat the oven to 190oC/gas mark 5
2. Whizz all the ingredients in a food processor until smooth, with no remaining lumps.
3. Pour the sponge into a pre-lined baking tray, spread evenly — 1cm thick — with a spatula and bake at 190oC for 15 minutes.
4. Check with a toothpick, that when it is inserted into the centre, it comes out clean. Allow to cool.

Agar Agar Mix

- 1 tsp agar agar powder or 1 tbsp agar flakes
- 240g water

METHOD

1. 1. Dissolve the agar agar in the water. Bring to the boil whisking continuously, keep it boiling for another 20 seconds. Store in the fridge.

Reduced Aquafaba

Aquafaba is the water from a chickpea can. To work properly as egg white substitute, it has to be reduced.

METHOD

1. Pour the water of a chickpea can into a saucepan, gently simmer on medium heat until it has reduced by about 40%. (If the water of a chickpea can has an average weight of 180g, it should be reduced to +/- 100g). Reduced aquafaba can be stored in the fridge or the freezer.

Flaxseed Mix

- 10g flaxseeds
- 30g cold water

METHOD

1. Mix the flaxseeds with the water and let it rest for at least 15 minutes, or until it gets a thick purée consistency. Can be kept in the fridge or freezer.

Tempering Chocolate

This is a long, complex but fascinating story! To make it simple, tempering is the process of gently heating and cooling chocolate to stabilise the emulsification of cocoa solids and fats. It is a crucial operation to avoid the chocolate melting in your hands or quickly turning white. A tempered chocolate can be kept for weeks at room temperature without losing its shiny and crispy texture.

Among different methods to melt the chocolate, the microwave is the easiest and quickest one, as long as you know your microwave! This is why I always recommend to melt the chocolate 10 or 15 seconds at a time. Chocolates should be melted at 40–45oC. To bring the temperature down, add some chocolate chips — one third of the initial weight. Stir with a wooden spoon. You should reach 32oC for dark chocolate, 30oC for vegan milk alternative and 28oC for vegan white alternative.

Raising Agents

Baking soda: Also called sodium bicarbonate. Combined with moisture and an acidic ingredient, it helps baked goods to rise. As the reaction begins immediately, recipes calling for baking soda should be baked immediately.

Apple cider vinegar: Healthier, quality alternative to other vinegars. Usage in vegan baking: the acid breaks down protein and helps to lighten the mix. Reacts nicely with baking soda.

Baking powder: Baking powder contains baking soda (sodium bicarbonate) and a dry acid (cream of tartar). When liquid is added to a baking recipe, these two ingredients react to form bubbles of carbon dioxide gas, making the cake batter or bread dough rise.

Instant yeast and active dry yeast: The difference between these 2 types of dry yeast is simple: Active dry yeast has a larger granule and needs to be dissolved in a liquid (water, milk) before using, while instant yeast has a finer texture and can be mixed right into the dry ingredients.

Fats and Oils

Coconut oil: Extremely nutritious fat that can be found in the flesh of the coconut. It is a rich alternative to butter with a smooth texture. Coconut oil is solid at room temperature which makes it great for baking.
Unrefined coconut oil has a coconut flavour, while refined coconut oil does not.

Rapeseed oil: Also called "British olive oil", is my favourite oil for Vegan desserts. Especially recommended for its health benefits, low in saturated fat, high in omegas 3-6-9 and a leading source of protein. It is one of the only unblended oils that can be heated to a high frying temperature without losing its character, colour or flavour. Its very mild taste is highly appreciated in Vegan baking, as it doesn't affect the taste of the dessert.

Vegan margarine or spread: The butter alternative you will choose will depend on the recipe. Among the brands found in the supermarkets I would recommend Vitalite, dairy-free spread: its texture makes it work for most of the pastries, cakes and creams. Nevertheless, a puff pastry will require a firmer vegan margarine. Same for some light "butter creams". The Naturli brand, organic vegan block gives very good results.

Thickeners

Agar agar: Agar Agar, also known as vegetable gelatine, is a vegan gelling agent derived from seaweed. Agar usually comes in three forms: powder, flakes, or a bar. Powdered Agar is usually recommended, as it dissolves more easily than flakes or bars. One advantage of Agar is that it sets at room temperature. If your recipe doesn't give you a measurement, you can follow this rule of thumb: to thicken 1 cup (240ml) of liquid, use 1 teaspoon Agar powder, or 1 tablespoon Agar flakes. The Agar solution should always be brought to the boil and simmered for 20–30 seconds.

Cornflour: Also called maizena. Very fine starch powder derived from maize (US corn) used in cooking as a thickener, to keep things from sticking, and provide an elastic texture.

Arrowroot: Arrowroot powder is a type of starch that can be used instead of cornflour in many ways, including baking, but is most appreciated as a thickener of liquids because it makes sparkling clear jellies, whereas using cornflour always gives cloudy results.
Use very little in a recipe: half the required quantity of cornflour.

Xanthan Gum: Is a flavourless thickener, often used in gluten-free baking as a replacement for the sticky effect of gluten.

Sweeteners

Sugar: BROWN SUGARS are quite often used in sweet baking. Certain recipes require specific brown sugars: light or dark muscovado sugar for a sticky toffee pudding, light or dark brown soft sugar for fruit cakes, demerara sugar for crumble toppings... Golden caster sugar is a fine sugar that is ideal for use in creamed sponge cakes.
WHITE SUGARS are refined brown sugars. They taste sweeter than their counterparts. Caster sugar is finer than granulated sugar and dissolves more easily, making it ideal for cakes, custards and mousses. It's also perfect for snowy white meringues. Icing sugar is a white sugar ground to a fine powder with the addition of cornflour. It dissolves on contact with liquid and is therefore used to sweeten foods that are not going to be heated. It is also used for dusting cakes and desserts. When choosing which sugar to bake with, preferably look for unrefined, organic or vegan brands.

Corn syrup: Is pressed directly from corn kernels and is almost as sweet as the granulated sugar it often replaces in recipes. The use of light corn syrup is recommended when a cream needs to remain white and glossy (see the coconut whipped cream). Also often used in sweet making because of its resistance to crystallisation.

Agave syrup: Also known as agave nectar is a natural, unrefined liquid sweetener extracted from the Mexican agave plant. It has a much lower glycaemic index than conventional sugar.

Brown rice syrup: A sweetener that is rich in compounds categorised as sugars, and is derived from cooked rice starch.

Maple syrup: Pure maple syrup is a natural, unrefined liquid sweetener, rich in trace minerals. Gives a nutty flavour to your cakes and creams.

Coconut sugar: Coconut sugar is a natural sugar derived from the liquid sap of the coconut blossoms. It has a low glycaemic index, is less refined and processed than other powdered sugars and far more nutritious. Adds a rich caramel flavour to a dessert.

Egg Substitutes

Aquafaba: This is the water from a chickpea can and it replaces egg whites. It works perfectly well for meringues. To give its best results it has to be reduced to get the same consistency as an egg white. Explained in the Basics. I think the person who, one day, discovered these virtues of chickpea water deserves a Nobel prize or, at least, a gold medal!

Cashew butter: Replaces the egg yolks in creams (custard). 1 tsp cashew butter replaces 1 egg yolk.

Flax seeds and chia seeds: Use 1 tbsp of ground flax seeds or chia seeds + 3 tbsp of water to replace 1 egg. Stir together and let it set until the mix thickens, about 15 minutes. Works perfectly for sponges and cake batters. Can be kept in the fridge or freezer.

Mashed fruits: Mashed bananas give a fruity taste to your sponges. Count ½ banana for 1 egg. Mashed avocado unlike the bananas are flavourless and will give a smooth texture to your mousses. 1 tbsp mashed avocado will replace 1 egg.

Silken tofu: Adds moisture to a recipe, ideal for mousses and cremes brulées. It has to be drained in a muslin and puréed before you use, to avoid chunks in the final product. About 60g drained silken tofu replaces 1 egg.

Vegan egg powder: Combination of starches and leavening ingredients. Among all the egg replacers I have been trying, "Follow your heart" gives the best results, especially for the choux pastry.

Cornflour, potato starch, arrowroot: Work as a binder in recipes.

Baking soda + apple cider vinegar: Mix 1 tsp of baking soda with 1 tsp of apple cider vinegar to replace 1 egg. It will add some fluffy, airiness to the sponges and cake batters.
Coconut vinegar has a similar effect.

Non-Dairy Products

Non-dairy milks: There are many varieties of non-dairy milks including soy, almond, rice, coconut… I have a preference for the KoKo dairy free coconut milk. It's very mild and neutral taste, does not affect the flavour of the dessert. Available in an original, light or unsweetened version. Rice milk is a great alternative for people suffering from a nut allergy.

Non-dairy cream cheeses: Nowadays, the market offers multiple choices. Various brands present different textures, from soft till extra firm. A firm cream cheese alternative — such as the KoKo dairy free — will always give better results in a cheesecake recipe or a cupcake frosting.

Non-dairy creams: Among diverse cream alternatives, oat cream is highly recommended for its very mild and neutral taste.

Food Colouring

Always check the label when using a food colouring. I would recommend "Watson and Web cake decorating colours" and "PME 100% Natural Food Colouring", both vegan friendly. The first one is available on Amazon. The second one can be found on Amazon and in Lakeland stores.

Chocolates

Again, always read carefully the components of the chocolates: a dark chocolate very often contains milk or buttermilk! A specifically vegan brand is recommended to remain on the safe side. Many brands are available nowadays.

Equipment

Food processor: Is the workhorse of the kitchen. Can be used for puréeing, blending, chopping nuts...

Blender: Ideal for smoothies, ice cream bases...

Stand or Hand mixer: Essential for pastries, meringues, yeast doughs... For an intensive use, it is worth investing in a heavy-duty model (Kitchen Aid, Kenwood) A light hand electric mixer is perfect for small quantities.

Microwave: As long as you know your microwave, this appliance will be a precious help to melt or reheat your creams and ingredients. Always read your manual before starting, as all microwaves don't necessarily have the same wattage.
A general guide would be:
Low power - 160W - to reheat mixes or soften ice creams.
Medium power - 350W - to melt vegan spreads, oils or chocolates.
Medium-high power - 500W- milk alternatives, creams and coconut cream.
Full power - 750W - reheating food with a water content (e.g. agar agar mix).

Scale: An electronic platform scale, 3 or 5 kg will ensure accurate measurements.

Silpat: A silicone non-stick reusable baking mat. Can be used for the oven and the freezer. Parchment paper is adequate for lining cake tins and baking trays.

Silicone moulds: All kind of shapes, nowadays at affordable prices, they will introduce fantasy and creativity in your desserts.

Thermometer: Is a must if you want to make caramel, Italian meringue, pate de fruits or temper chocolate.

Baking sheets and cake pans: Come in all different shapes and sizes. Among them you will need 3 baking sheets at least, a 12-piece muffin pan, a loose-bottom springform tin, minutei savarin moulds...

Pastry tools: A hardwood rolling pin, a pastry brush, a straight and an angled palette knife, knives, spatulas, whisks, scissors. Piping bags, plain and star nozzles. Heavy bottom saucepans. Sieve and muslin.

Useful Website Addresses and Suppliers

Dairy free products
www.kokodairyfree.com

Pastry ingredients and Equipment
www.homechocolatefactory.com
The biggest range of silicone moulds
www.classicfinefoods.co.uk
All natural essences, rising agents, thickeners…
www.nisbets.co.uk
All basic equipment. Different stores in London.

Vegan Chocolates
www.plamilfoods.co.uk/chocolate
Good variety of dark, milk and white vegan chocolate alternatives.
Affordable prices with their bulk options.

www.homechocolatefactory.com
Launched a wide range of vegan chocolates. Their latest white chocolate
alternative is just amazing!

Edible flowers
www.victoriananursery.co.uk
All colours and varieties, seeds or plants.

Vegan colours
www.amazon.co.uk (Beetroot powder, PME 100% Natural, Watson and
Webb cake decorating colours

Coconut milk, evaporated and condensed milk
www.wingyipstore.co.uk

Vegan Egg powder
www.followyourheart.com

Index

ACKNOWLEDGMENTS

When I first came up with the idea of a Vegan Pastry Cookbook, it was as if I was trying to reach the moon: "You have no chance, you are not famous, you don't have thousands of followers…"

I persisted and sent my manuscript to a few publishers.

Three weeks later, I had an answer from the Olympia Publishers, I was in heaven!

So, I would like to thank everyone at Olympia Publishing and especially Jake Molton, James Houghton, Kristina Smith, Chantelle Wadsworth and Katie Major for their interest in my work.

Desserts are always caught by the eyes first, and they wouldn't look so delicious without the extraordinary talent of Darrin Jenkins, my food photographer.

I also would like to thank Sam Platt and the Vegetarian Society team. They have shown fantastic support from the very beginning, always interested and enthusiastic about my new ideas and projects!

Not to forget Tim, Alan, Pete and the VegFest team, Karin Ridgers and her VeggievisionTV who always welcomed me to their shows. And all these discreet and helpful friends, Anne, Linda, Heather, Lizzy, Lucy and so many others whom, I am sure, will recognise themselves.

Also, a special thanks to The Avenue Cookery School for offering me the opportunity to give my favourite Vegan Pastry trainings!

Last, but not least, I have to thank my family, and especially my heroic husband who had to taste tons of desserts, at any hour of the day.

Merci Daniel!